PUBLIC SPEAKING

How to Prepare and Deliver a Speech With Charisma

(How to Develop Self-confidence, Beat Social Anxiety and Influence People by Public Speaking)

Carmine Acker

Published by Rob Miles

© **Carmine Acker**

All Rights Reserved

Public Speaking: How to Prepare and Deliver a Speech With Charisma (How to Develop Self-confidence, Beat Social Anxiety and Influence People by Public Speaking)

ISBN 978-1-7771171-8-4

All rights reserved. No part of this guide may be reproduced in any form without permission in writing from the publisher except in the case of brief quotations embodied in critical articles or reviews.

Legal & Disclaimer

The information contained in this book is not designed to replace or take the place of any form of medicine or professional medical advice. The information in this book has been provided for educational and entertainment purposes only.

The information contained in this book has been compiled from sources deemed reliable, and it is accurate to the best of the Author's knowledge; however, the Author cannot guarantee its accuracy and validity and cannot be held liable for any errors or omissions. Changes are periodically made to this book. You must consult your doctor or get professional medical advice before using any of the suggested remedies, techniques, or information in this book.

Upon using the information contained in this book, you agree to hold harmless the Author from and against any damages, costs, and expenses, including any legal fees potentially resulting from the application of any of the information provided by this guide. This disclaimer applies to any damages or injury caused by the use and application, whether directly or indirectly, of any advice or information presented, whether for breach of contract, tort, negligence, personal injury, criminal intent, or under any other cause of action.

You agree to accept all risks of using the information presented inside this book. You need to consult a professional medical practitioner in order to ensure you are both able and healthy enough to participate in this program.

Table of Contents

INTRODUCTION 1

CHAPTER 1: THE PARTS OF A SPEECH (& AN IN-DEPTH LOOK AT EACH PART) 3

CHAPTER 2: HUMANKIND FEELS FIRST THROUGH THE SENSUAL PORTRAITS 15

CHAPTER 3: "P-O-P" YOUR PSYCHOLOGICAL FEAR BUBBLE 22

CHAPTER 4: PUBLIC SPEAKING 101AND MORE 26

CHAPTER 5: WHAT IS COMMUNICATION 29

CHAPTER 6: BE AT YOUR BEST IN PUBLIC SPEAKING 46

CHAPTER 7: A HEALTHY RELATIONSHIP THROUGH COMMUNICATION 54

CHAPTER 8: THE GOAL THAT MAKES YOUR AUDIENCE LOVE YOUR TALK 58

CHAPTER 9: KNOW THE BEST PRESENTATION STRUCTURE 62

CHAPTER 10: HOW PUBLIC SPEAKING CAN HELP YOUR CAREER 74

CHAPTER 11: TALKING WITH ANYONE –WHAT DO YOU NEED? 78

CHAPTER 12: BOOT CAMP: PREPARING YOURSELF 82

CHAPTER 13: HOW TO STRUCTURE YOUR SPEECH 93

CHAPTER 14: THE POWER OF EXAMPLES IN PUBLIC SPEAKING 114

CHAPTER 15: FEAR OF PUBLIC SPEAKING 122

CHAPTER 16: TECHNICALITIES 135

CHAPTER 17: GETTING STARTED 152

CHAPTER 18: FEAR TECHNOLOGY 174

CONCLUSION 177

Introduction

This book contains proven steps and strategies on how to rock the stage as you deliver your speech in front of a crowd. Now there's no more reason to faint at the thought of presenting your thoughts in public because, with the help of this book, you will learn a multitude of techniques in order to finally make public speaking a comfortable art to engage in.

This book will teach you the power of public speech and the role that it plays in our everyday lives. We aren't really aware of it, but we actually engage in public speaking every day. This is the exact reason why you shouldn't treat it as a physical threat, one that is foreign and unknowable. Equipped with tips on how to overcome and win against your fear of talking in public, this book will also guide you on what steps you should take before you hold onto that microphone.

It's very easy to understand and you will find insights on the proper behavior that you must observe while you face your audience. Even how your voice should sound is discussed here. Talk about specific!

As public speaking is a skill that would provide you with great advantage in today's competitive world, the understandable and easy manner that this book uses in order to explain the intricacies of public speaking will help you reach your goal of finally becoming a confident and able public speaker.

Thanks again for downloading this book. I hope you enjoy it!

Chapter 1: The Parts Of A Speech (& An In-Depth Look At Each Part)

According to Wikipedia, public speaking is defined as "... giving a lecture to a group of people in a structured, deliberate manner intended to inform, influence, or entertain." **It goes on to state that** "most of the time, public speaking is to persuade the audience."

There are basically three reasons to give a speech:

1) To tell a story or to entertain, both of which should have a point,

2) To present information, and

3) To convince people about something (which includes selling).

In any of these cases, each speech in its simplest sense, a speech has basically five parts: (1) an introduction whereby the speaker explains why they are giving the talk, (2) an opening statement which introduces the topic and explains its relevance, (3) a quick overview which gives the audience an idea of what to expect, (4) the main body of the speech, itself, (5) a conclusion and/or a brief summary.

In a lecture setting, this is often followed by a question and answer session. This is yet another reason to make sure you really understand the subject matter you are presenting.

An actual speech, however, is a lot more complicated than that. While the aforementioned parts of a speech should be followed in that order, there are other things you also have to consider when making your speech. Let's take an in-depth look at each part:

1) THE INTRODUCTION

If people are going to listen to you talk, they want to know who you are that they should listen to you. Why, for example, would you attend a speech on finding your soul mate from a spinster? It's like listening to weight loss advice from someone who obviously shops at the super-size section of a clothing store, isn't it?

Your audience wants to know how qualified you are to talk about the subject at hand. Even when you are introduced by a moderator, you should add something to what they say in order to **establish your credibility**.

This is extremely important, because unless you come across as credible, you will lose your audience even before your speech begins. You can talk and talk, discuss the secrets of the universe, even — but once your audience shuts you out, you might as well be alone. Worse, you could find yourself rejected and have to face wild beasts by yourself.

While credibility is important, however, you can still lose your audience if you don't explain how your credentials can serve them. For this, you need a hook, which will be discussed next.

2) OPENING STATEMENT WITH A HOOK

The opening statement tells your audience what the topic is all about. While it's very likely that they already know what it is, it's important that you reiterate it, anyway. To avoid insulting them, however, be sure to paraphrase it. Otherwise, they'll get the impression that you're just going to read out an entire script to them, which will turn them off.

If your topic is about... ooh, how to give a speech, for example, then don't say something like: "**Today, I'm going to teach you how to give a speech**."

Remember, there's a good chance they already know why they're sitting in front of you. This is where the hook comes in. Whether you are trying to convince people to believe in something, or to do something, or even to buy something, their mental bottom line will always be: **What's In It For Me?**

A: "Clean your room!"

B: "Why? What's in it for me?"

A: "Believe in god!"

B: "Why? What's in it for me?"

A: "Buy this!"

B: "Why? What's in it for me?"

In other words, we are all rather selfish and self-centered individuals. The hook, therefore, is the lure to draw people in, the thing which answers the burning question of "**What's in it for me?**" or WIIFM.

"**Today, I'm going to teach you how to give a speech,**" qualifies as an opening statement, but it is a boring one.

"**When was the last time you had to give a speech and wished you were invisible?**" is a much better opening statement. It tells them that you're human, that you have a sense of humor, that you understand how dreadful public speaking can be, and that you've been there before. This last bit further reinforces your credibility and justifies why you are the one standing up, and not sitting among your audience. Because you've been in their shoes, but made it through to the other side.

"Well, what if I could teach you how to do it easily and in a way that feels pretty fun?" **is your hook.**

That hook draws them in and tells them they are in the right place. To make it more effective, however, you need to make it both personal and emotional.

"Whether you're giving a talk in class, selling a product, or forced to give a speech like this; wouldn't it be great if you could do it easily, effectively, and without fear?"

This hook should come shortly after you give your credentials. With so many professionals out there, your hook tells them why **you** are different and what **you** specifically can do for **them**.

You'll be dealing with a diverse audience, so you have to cast as wide a net as you can. The more personalized and relevant you can make your opening statement and hook, the greater the chances of holding on to them till the end of your speech.

3) THE OVERVIEW

Once you've hooked your audience, you should then give them an outline of what your speech will cover. If your speech is only a few minutes long, you can dispense with this. If it is longer, or if you are trying to teach something, then the overview is essential. This is also true if you are trying to convince them about something.

Think of the overview as a kind of table of contents. By letting your audience know where you're going, it keeps them from getting lost.

It also prevents interruptions. In the overview of **this** book, I explained the topics to be covered, which includes handling nervousness. Were you hearing this in a speech, my overview would let you know that I **will** cover that issue, and at exactly what point.

A good overview is not only brief, but it should also keep the speaker from losing their stride because of hands constantly going up in the air. It also ensures that the audience stays focused on the speaker's message instead of getting distracted because they're wondering if the speaker will cover an issue they're interested in.

If you are making a speech to entertain or to inspire, an overview becomes unnecessary. Entertaining and inspirational speeches often have greater impact when they seem unrehearsed and extemporaneous.

4) MAIN BODY OF THE SPEECH

You **really** need to do your research. When writing your information down, however, **only** write out the main points, in bullet-point or list format. Do not make the mistake of writing it all out in paragraph style to read aloud.

Think in terms of main points and lists, not in terms of a body. Doing so forces you to keep it simple, allowing you to direct the flow of your message in an orderly manner. Seeing **only** the main points, you can also spot and eliminate repetitious topics (which tends to bore people to death).

Remember: if your audience wanted to read something, they certainly don't need you to narrate. And if they wanted to hear a recording, the **last** thing they'd attend is a live speech.

The greatest advantage to writing down main points in a list format instead of huge chunks of text, is that you don't have to memorize anything. Actors who freeze on stage sometimes do so because they forget their lines. If you understand your topic and forget something, simply refer to your notes and let the information flow.

5) CONCLUSION AND SUMMARY

Many people confuse conclusions with summaries, an error you must not make. A conclusion provides the answer or closure to the things you've covered, while a summary is a recap of what you've discussed (which typically includes the conclusion).

Your conclusion should be something like, "Because of A and B, I believe that C is the obvious result. To summarize, therefore..."

If you discussed three points in your speech, for example, the summary would reiterate all those points at the end. You would say something along the lines of, **"So to recap: this is point A, then point B, and therefore, here's C. The end."** That's your summary.

If your speech is short, a summary is unnecessary, so you can go ahead to your conclusion. Informative speeches tend to be longer, however, requiring a review of what you've already discussed.

A summary is not meant to be a repetition of your speech! It only very briefly reiterates the information you've already presented. If there's going to be a question and answer portion, it can even remind your audience of a question they may have wanted to ask but forgot about.

Note: In cases where the relationship between your information and your conclusion is **less clear**, you might want to present the summary **before** presenting your conclusion. This way, you make sure that your audience is still with you **before** you lead them to your final point. It also ensures that they can follow the relationship between your information and whatever it is you have concluded.

In such cases (hopefully when most of your audience goes "**aah!**"), you can then summarize the entire thing, once more. This is not meant to be repetitive, but to ensure your audience really got it. This is rare, however. Worse, it means you have not presented your information clearly enough, or that you're addressing an audience that's not qualified enough to fully understand your speech.

Words to use when concluding are: in conclusion, all things considered, from the final analysis, finally, therefore, **etc.**

Words to use during your summary can include: all in all, briefly, by and large, in brief, overall, in short, in summary, in the long run, to summarize, **etc.**

While not always possible, it's also recommended that you relate your conclusion to your audience. If you were giving a speech on how to give a great speech, for example, then state that they should now become better speech makers while trying to obtain their agreement... yes? (in the form of nodding)

Chapter 2: Humankind Feels First

Through The Sensual Portraits

What words compel a person to accomplish things in life that surpass the ability of their contemporaries? What words drive the ordinary to become the extraordinary? What words transform the broken, bewildered, and lost soul to see the light and turn the course of their personal human history away from drugs, crime, abuse, and myriad plagues of the human condition? What words congeal the convictions of a nation to stand strong in tragedy and, as President Lincoln acclaimed, appeal to the "better angels of our nature"? What words compel a people to unite and overthrow the oppressor, to repel the aggressor, to rescue the destitute? They are words that stir our inner being, convict our souls, and move our spirits. They are neither accidental nor random; they are honed and tempered in the fires of human adversity and experience.

They are words spoken in season, arising from the depths of the messenger, cascading so strongly to the surface that they will not be contained. They are words that flood the messenger's soul, consume their waking moments, and compel them so strongly that failing to speak, they would die and shrivel inside. The great prophets, clerics, political leaders, civil rights leaders, and orators of history use the language of their generation to capture the minds and hearts of thousands. Their words evoke the angels of our soul, trigger strong emotion, and evoke action.

I have noted in my observations of world class and world champion speakers that they prevail upon and compel our soul when they reveal and expose a piece of their own. **Messages that Matter,** are first and foremost the words that matter to us. They are what each of as an individual person hold closely as our treasure. They are the pearls of great price occupying the treasure trove of our personal faith. Faith being the belief structure upon which our life is built, the principles laid as steel and stone, mortar and mesh, the very framework of our lives, and tempered with a lifetime of experiences and people who have helped construct our being. For with each principle laid in our temporal house, we can go back to a person or event that hewed it, forged it, chipped away at it, and placed it into our being by adversity or admiration.

Emotion is the secret passage to the heart of an audience. Not the soppy, sloppy, drivel of cheap romance novels; rather, emotion is the tugging, tearing, treacherous minefield of human thinking—the revelation of the human soul from one being to another. The words that evoke emotional response, challenge beliefs, upset the comfortable repose of settled thoughts, blowing open parts of the mind that are notable in their reclusive resolve.

Evoke emotion and you awaken thought. The higher order brain has wakened its slumbering librarian to send her racing through the stacks to look up forgotten memories, junior high formulas, high school and college experiences, slights and hurts, moments of weakness and strength. Emotion scurries between the visual and aural arts, psychology, music, and speech. Emotion claims vocabulary definitions, applies ancient rules and codes, analyzing contrasting concepts, synthesizing information from different Dewey Decimal locations to create new conclusions, new learning. Emotion is a conduit connecting sensual input and output to arrive at judgment.

Words that matter make us emote as a precursor to action. Words that matter conduct a symphony in our minds, plucking the strings, pounding the drums, bringing life into our orchestra pit. Emotion connects to people and events in our life that make us think. Words cast on the movie screen of our mind the images from our life that compel us to act differently, or act at all to correct or compel the events that make this world a better place or launch us into the abyss.

Immortal speakers touch our emotions like a winemaker pushes open the oaken doors to deep cellars and enters, lumbering down into the recesses of our deepest thoughts and beliefs. He calls to attention those principles from our faith and making them new, making them purposeful, moves us up and out to walk in a new light. We understand that words have changed us when they have combined with thoughts and experiences of a lifetime. Words that matter bring truth into focus. Not all truth. Not another's truth. They reveal our truth! The truth that makes us who we are. The truth that compels our life.

Immortal speakers engage our emotions. To do that, they must master the craft of speaking to our hearts first and our heads second. Touch the emotions to open the door. This is done with words—words well spoken, spoken from the heart compelling the world to listen, to listen to the evolution of principles birthed in their mind. 1. Immortal speakers understand they must speak from a unique blend of heart and head to capture their audience. They know that if you speak only from the heart, you are perceived as a fanatic. Speak only from your head and you are perceived as an academic, but speak from the heart and head and you will be authentic.

Immortal speakers learn the craft of speaking and writing words to be spoken in their own voice. It is a lifetime pursuit. For many of us, it is an elusive, rewarding quest for words to be spoken at the precise moment in history when the Earth is most vulnerable to being pushed off its axis by a heart and mind resolved to be different.

Immortal speakers are the message; their message is written on the tablets of their own human heart. "Men may be cowed by power, but they can only be converted by love." 2. In reality, strong emotion can turn the hearts of humankind for good or ill. Vitriolic movements in the soul of humankind change the personality and propel an individual in action or reaction never to be exactly the same again—words matter and energize human evolution.

"Death and life are in the power of the tongue and those who love it will eat its fruit" Proverbs 18:21 (NKJV).

Chapter 3: "P-O-P" Your Psychological Fear Bubble

"Why me?"

This is usually the first question asked by those who dislike public speaking once invited to present.

Then they cry.

They don't usually cry. That was a joke, but people do wonder, "Why me?" when they get asked to speak. Maybe they want to cry sometime. But they always wonder, "Why me?" Then fear sets in. Fear of failure. Fear of embarrassment. Fear of poor delivery. Fear of whatever you fear. This section will "POP" your fear bubble.

How do you rid yourself of fear? POP it. You must view the opportunity to speak as a Privilege (the first P). You must bring your Originality to your presentation (the O). You must be fully Present (the final P) from the minute you step on stage. Let's explore how this looks.

The first P is to view your invitation to speak as a privilege. You have the privilege of sharing knowledge. You have been chosen to speak because you have something to teach the audience. This simple shift in your perspective will help you overcome fright and anxiety. Your presentation no longer requires you to entertain your audience with charm and rhetoric alone. Instead, it is an opportunity to teach what you have learned. This answers your "Why you?" question. You were asked to speak because you have something to teach.

The O stands for originality. You have been asked to speak because the audience and organizers believe in your message and in you. The key is to recognize they want to learn from you. You must bring your original and authentic self to the meeting, event, or speaking opportunity. Your personality, your experiences, your findings must lead the presentation. You do not have to be anyone else. You do not have to pretend to be anyone else. If they wanted someone else, they would not be paying you. As you prepare your remarks, contemplate how the audience will describe your presentation style. Do you want to be funny, self-deprecating, transparent, calming, energizing, hopeful, light-hearted, provocative? Each speech will be different, but stay close to your core personality. This allows you to feel more comfortable presenting. It also allows your audience to experience a heightened sense of connectivity to your genuine nature.

The final P is Presence. You must bring your complete presence and energy from the first moment you begin your remarks, presentation, or training. Most speakers fail here. I have coached dozens of people who believed the purpose of their first three minutes of a speech was to warm up, work out the nerves, and then get into "the groove." This is the wrong approach. Your audience wants your complete presence. They want it now. Before I go on stage, I take three deep breaths. Others watch stand up comedy videos, listen to their favorite songs, meditate, or jump up and down. You can find your own approach to ensure you are energized, engaged, and fully present the moment you begin your presentation. If you are not, your audience will feel it.

Chapter 4: Public Speaking 101 and More

What is the biggest fear most people have? According to one of the world's leading top personal development and public speaking coaches, Brian Tracy, the average person fears public speaking even more than death itself . . .

It is important to understand that being able to effectively communicate your ideas is absolutely critical when it comes to making decisions, hiring and directing teammates, speaking effectively with employees and staff, and is a major skill when it comes to the promotion of ideas and bringing people to these ideas.

Good public speaking can help you be successful with promoting new business ideas, organizing and managing businesses through team leadership, giving presentations to promote ideas and even push social issues as well as creating highly effective presentations people want to see.

The good news for beginners is that public speaking all comes down to a set of learnable skills that can be practiced and improved upon.

Most people are capable of giving reasonable public presentations with just a few hours of practice. In this guide we are going to discuss that skill set as well as other tips, strategies and ideas that you can use to almost immediately improve your public speaking skills, and over time allow you to actually master this important skill.

I will discuss the skills in each section and how you can utilize them to build upon each other with overlapping support strategies that are easy to master and will greatly improve how you speak and present to people.

Remove Your Fear

Most people do NOT like having to learn and practice public speaking. It is important to remember that when you are learning public speaking skills, that you are in the exact same boat as everyone else. THEY don't like it either.

Consider public speaking much like learning how to play tennis. At first, you will be clumsy, miss the ball, feel like you have 10 thumbs on your hands, and you will stumble around and make plenty of mistakes. As you continue to practice, begin to hone your skills, and before you realize it, you begin to look, sound and actually feel significantly better when you are required to stand before any group and give a presentation.

The more quickly that you take control of your emotions and redirect your thinking so that you begin to learn public speaking skills, will help you master the entire process a lot quicker than if you allow negative emotions control your thinking. Keep continuing to practice speaking and following the other steps in this guide and you will quickly master the basics.

Chapter 5: What Is Communication

Communication comes from the Latin "communicare," which means "to make another participant of what one has." Communication is the action of communicating or communicating; it is understood as the process by which information is transmitted and received. Every human and animal being has the ability to communicate with others. But, for a communication process to take place, the presence of six elements is essential: that there be an issue; that is, someone who transmits the information; a receiver, someone to whom the information is directed and who receives it; and a communication channel, which can be oral or written.

WHAT IS COMMUNICATION

Communication is a way of exchanging information between a sender and a receiver, in which the first transmits the message and the second interprets and produces a response, if necessary. As regards human beings, communication is a psychic activity of its own, derived from thought, language, and the development of the psychosocial capacities of relationships.

Communication as a social value is the basis of personal and group self-affirmation since through it; we exchange opinions and feelings with other people. Learning to communicate is essential for the development of our personality. Therefore, above all, a conversation must be surrounded by sincerity and honesty.

Through the word, we communicate our thoughts and feelings and establish personal relationships with our family, friends, at school, at work, and in the community. Therefore, every day, we must strive more to achieve perfection in communication skills: speaking, listening, writing, and reading.

TYPES OF COMMUNICATION

People communicate with each other in different ways that depend upon the message and its context in which it is being sent. Choice of communication channel and your style of communicating also affect communication. So, there are a variety of types of communication.

Types of communication-based on the communication channels used are:

Verbal Communication

Nonverbal Communication

VERBAL COMMUNICATION

Verbal Communication is all kinds of passage or exchange of information through language written or spoken.

The success of Verbal Communication depends completely on the clarity of past messages, and this clarity is linked to the compatibility of the vocabulary and intellectual collection of those involved in the exchange of information. For Verbal Communication to be successful, whether written or spoken, the recipient of the message must understand what he reads or hears, for this, the message must be in a code common to the sender and receiver (same language), and both are on the same level of knowledge. When any of these essential conditions fails, there is what is called noise in communication.

Despite the great technological advances, Verbal Communication is still the most used to pass information, especially in interpersonal relationships. In one company, for example, notices are given in written language, e-mail is still the most widely used web-based messaging feature, and in family relationships, dialogue remains effective. Although Visual Communication is today the most used feature in advertising, it still uses verbal resources in some media, such as radio and television, and eventually the Internet.

Some resources used in Verbal Communication are responsible for attaching the receiver's attention to the message, such as impact and curiosity.

When a message is sent, the sender must have the least sensitivity to know the effect it will have on the receiver. When the effect is impactful, it generates a correspondence with the receiver's experience, and this sharpens him to pay more attention to the message he is receiving. Therefore, the receiver's curiosity is fundamental for the message sent by the sender to have the desired effect.

Verbal Communication is further divided into:

Oral Communication

Written Communication

Oral communication is that which is established between two or more people using a language or code-shared through a means of physical transmission, which was traditionally the air, although today we can add the phone or videoconference.

Oral communication allows us to transmit the person with whom we speak information, ideas, feelings, emotions, beliefs, opinions, attitudes, etc.

To carry out oral communication, we use the voice to reproduce the sounds of the language, form words, and elaborate messages that contain the information we want to transmit to our interlocutor.

For oral communication to take place there must be at least two people involved who perform, alternatively, the role of the sender (who delivers the information) and receiver (who receives it).

The transmitted information is known as a message. This message is prepared according to a system of linguistic sounds corresponding to code or language.

The message is transmitted through a physical medium, which can be the air, but it can also be a telecommunications device, such as a telephone or a computer.

The process of oral communication, in turn, is framed within a context that can influence the meaning or meaning of the message: the place, the situation and the circumstance in which it is delivered, see how it is received. And interpret.

Oral communication is characterized by being spontaneous, developing on the fly, being direct and straightforward, by resorting to body language to reinforce or emphasize the message (gestures, attitudes, postures), for being dynamic and immediate.

Oral communication is characteristic of the human being and is established in all areas in which it relates and needs to communicate: from the personal to the professional, from the political to the economic or commercial.

Examples of oral communication are given daily: a conversation, a talk, a conference, a speech, an interview, a master class, a debate, are quite common oral communication situations.

TYPES OF ORAL COMMUNICATION

Spontaneous oral communication

Spontaneous oral communication is one that does not meet a previously established plan, theme, or structure, but is developed in the form of a dialogue between two or more people. An example of spontaneous oral communication is an informal conversation.

Planned oral communication

The planned oral communication is one that obeys a previously drawn plan, with guidelines, themes, or structures designed in advance. This plan will guide the communication process so that it is carried out within certain defined limits. This type of communication can be, in turn, of two kinds: multidirectional and unidirectional.

Multidirectional

The planned oral communication is multidirectional when, within its interaction guidelines, it establishes the intervention of several interlocutors who offer their different opinions and approaches on a previously defined topic or issue. An example of this type of communication can be a debate.

Unidirectional

We speak of unidirectional planned oral communication when it involves only one broadcaster who addresses an audience to expose a topic or issue extensively. Examples of unidirectional communication are speeches, conferences, or master classes.

Written communication is a type of communication that man has that allows him to express himself through a piece of paper or for his part today can be done by means of a computer. In other words, written communication can be described as the method we use to communicate but in a written way ; In this, the issuer (individual who issues the message) prepares different types of texts or writings such as novels, written works, newspaper articles, stories, research papers, analysis, among others, since with them he seeks to transmit his message which can reach an undetermined number of recipients (people who accept or receive the message).

Written communication can be distinguished from oral communication because it is not subject to time or space ; This means that this communication that is established between a sender and a receiver does not happen imminently or even may never occur, so that writing lasts until eternity, and this is one of the advantages and benefits of written communication. Which can be classified as permanent since it does not fade or forget like words, it can also reach much more people than oral communication.

Among the methods or types of communication, which include oral communication, gestural communication, and pictorial communication, written communication is one of the most used by man, in order to transmit each of his ideas, thoughts, and Knowledge through letters. It is important to mention that written communication makes it very possible for the person to be more expressive when writing a letter, or in turn increases its grammatical, lexical and syntactic complexity when it comes to engaging in oral communication with other individuals.

TYPES OF WRITTEN COMMUNICATION

Letter

It is the most personal form of communication that exists between communication modalities. Due to its nature, it allows the development of ideas without any rigor in the text, but always ensuring that there is coherence in the development of ideas regardless of whether this type of communication is intimate.

At this point, there are two common types of cards such as formal letters and informal letters. As its name advances, the formal ones are presented from an organization and can be written by that member of the organization that wishes to transmit a message according to their needs. In this case, there is a consensus on how it should be written both in the tone of the language and in the structure of the text itself.

The second type of letter is informal, and as the name implies, it is done by friends, family or anyone who wishes to convey a message from an intimate point of view and using a more colloquial language — of course, always taking care of the proper management and development of ideas.

Report

These types of texts allow the development of ideas in order to inform about what a particular person or group has requested. It is then sought, to disclose required information, to disseminate an event or to the analysis of an event, from the argumentative or numerical point of view through statistics.

The reports are classified according to their nature, from the public or private point of view, as the case may be. The formats that develop this type of texts can be simple or complex according to the same information needs. You can add text, graphics, tables, and other types of content that help you achieve the goal of reporting satisfactorily.

Email

It is a means of communication of great validity. It is basically based on the optimization of a communication tool through the Internet in which the necessary messages can be sent. More than a text structure, we are here with a means of communication.

Memorandum

It is a formal document, which presents specific reports or messages that seek to be taken into consideration on a specific date and defined in the memorandum itself. In it then, we will find a series of approaches that will be reviewed at the meeting that is agreed and accepted by the signatories that receive that text.

Minutes

This type of text is elaborated, specifically when work or business meeting is taking place. By its nature, it tries to be a document that at the end rescues and leaves present, all that type of subject and / or agreement that is developed in the said meeting.

In its final form, the minutes will be a document that presents a summary of what was said at that meeting and will also serve as an element of certification that the meeting was held in a timely manner.

Newspaper

This is considered as a means of mass written communication. The nature of the texts is basically to inform about a political, economic, social or any other event, depending on what is being sought.

NONVERBAL COMMUNICATION

Nonverbal communication refers to the action of communicating without speaking and is associated with emotional intelligence. Emotional intelligence is expressed through nonverbal communication, and this, through gestures, proximity, and sounds without words, manages to communicate assertively.

Types of nonverbal communication

Nonverbal communication is usually divided into three types of components:

the kinesic

the proxemic

paralinguistics

Kinesic nonverbal communication

Kinesic communication or body language corresponds to body gestures and looks. The word 'kinésico' comes from the Greek root, which means 'kinetic' or 'movement,' therefore; it encompasses the entire movement of the body.

Some examples of kinetic nonverbal communication are: raising eyebrows, standing in a triangle position, breathing rapidly, gaze positions, eye position, and winks.

Proxemics' nonverbal communication

Proxemics nonverbal communication refers to the distances a person is from another, communicating the proximity relationship between them.

The American anthropologist Edward T. Hall coined the term 'proxemics' and defined four types of interpersonal distances:

Intimate distance: 0 to 60 centimetres.

Personal distance: 6 0 to 120 centimetres.

Social distance: 120 to 300 centimetres.

Public distance: more than 300 centimetres.

The proxemics depends on the culture and also on how people use and respond to different types of spatial relationships, such as when someone wants to intimidate another person approaching beyond the comfort zone of the intimate person.

Nonverbal paralinguistic communication

Nonverbal paralinguistic communication is composed of oral, auditory, tactile and visual signs.

The paralinguistic elements are the expressions of sounds without words such as the growl; yawning; crying; Laughter; the tone or intensity and volume of the voice; intonation, accent and emphasis on speech; the slow, accelerated or stumbled rhythm of speaking; distortions or imperfections of speech among others.

Chapter 6: Be At Your Best In Public Speaking

Everyone can, and should, learn to speak well, in private or public arena. Why do we say so? Effective communication is the lifeblood of human relationship. Without a shared understanding of issues, no two persons can get along for long.

Again, if you look closely, you'd notice that many in the commanding heights of business, politics or social organisations, wormed their way to the top with the tool of knowing what to say, and how best to say it, to influence people and make them act in ways that advance the common good.

Granted that a few dumb asses could also buy, scheme or muscle their way up the ladder, but you certainly know many examples of people aided to the top by outstanding speech qualities. Barrack Obama readily comes to mind. A little known Illinois minority politician shot himself into national consciousness following an impactful keynote speech at the National Democratic Convention. He made it to the Senate and eventually clinched the topmost prize in global politics, as President of the United States.

In fact, it would appear awkward when a leader, in big or small communities or organisations, is unable to express himself well enough as to motivate, persuade or otherwise get people around him to understand him and act in a certain way. Agreed, fine speaking skill alone may not always take people to the top, or keep them there, if other leadership qualities are visibly absent. But, nobody can deny that it matters a great deal, to be able to speak in a way to touches the heart.

What about you?

Should you be interested in honing your skills in public speaking? Are you ever going to be called upon to make a speech on any important occasion? Your answer should be positive.

Let's not ignore the fact that everyone, including the deaf and dumb, communicates. We all must frequently need to share ideas and meanings with family members, friends, school mates or colleagues at work. The point is that we can always strive to improve the way we talk to people so that our message is easily understood and put to good use.

Yet, you may not see yourself as a public speaker. But, if three or more persons ever listened to you, for upward of five minutes, wouldn't you agree that you had already delivered a public speech? It's a misnomer to restrict the label to those who pay their bills by making speeches, on assorted topics, to varied audiences, around the country and beyond.

What's the point?

The point we're making is that effective communication skill is a quality that everyone should try to cultivate, no matter their calling or status in life. We agree that certain people rely more on it for the success of their careers, than others. For instance, politicians of all cadres must traverse their constituencies, speaking at one forum after another, as they strive to sell themselves and their ideas. They need to win hearts and votes in order to stay in business.

Motivational speakers live by talking and getting others to follow a certain cause. Successful religious entrepreneurs rake in huge sums in donations by talking. Yes, these all make more public speeches than the rest of us.

However, the fact that some people speak more than you, doesn't mean you do not speak at all! Or, that you should not bother to improve your skills in the art.

Why you should bother

Reason is, as we said earlier, there's hardly anyone who does not, once in a while, tell a story, convey a piece of information, share personal experience or, otherwise, speak to more than one person at a time. Picture in your mind, a family head instructing his wife and four children, after a meal. He qualifies as a public speaker. Yes, your audience could be family members, close friends, a few school mates or those in your work group.

Almost anyone could be called upon to make a speech before sizeable audiences, after a dinner, or at religious, social or business meetings.

In a sense, therefore, you, I and everyone could be a public speaker. We should be interested in speaking better and enjoying the fruitage of our lips. We should even speak more at critical times like the ones we currently live in, when racial hatred, religious bigotry and political strife cause mindless bloodletting in one place after another. Many should join the advocacy for tolerance and peaceful coexistence. So, the need for people to speak out has never been more urgent than it is now!

This booklet is carefully prepared, by the masters of the art, to help make the task of public speaking less daunting, wholly enjoyable and more effective.

With newbies in mind, we tried to keep it simple, practical and easy to follow. We have no doubt that even accomplished speakers will find a couple of things here that can oil a rusty part and help them do even better. After reading through, and if you try to follow its recommendations, you should be able to speak with appreciable ease. More importantly, you'd succeed in passing on the intended message and achieving the desired results.

You've got something to share!

We're taking it as given, that you really have something worthwhile to share with people. You can select an area of personal interest, arm yourself with current issues in the field and look for opportunities to influence people for positive change. You could share personal experience from which the audience could learn vital lessons; an idea of how to enhance an economic activity to make more money; how to make changes toward a healthier lifestyle; ways of improving marital or family relations to achieve peace and happiness, or how to make better political or social choices.

There's practically no end to what you can share with other persons. Keep in mind, though, that whatever you wish to share must be of importance to your audience. Otherwise, you'd be wasting their time, and yours, talking about trifles!

Your material could be written down, in full or in part. Or, it could be all there in your head, but you've got a clear mental outline of how to proceed. Let us quickly take you through the various steps that lead straight to the goal of a successful talk, one that leaves the listeners with a feeling of satisfaction; a readiness to take a certain action or accept a certain line of thought, in direct response to what is heard.

You'd notice that the book addresses, in great details, the essential ingredients of public speaking, including stage presence, voice control, body language and quality delivery. You'd also find useful answers to the frequently asked questions like, **how can I be a good public speaker** and **how does one prepare for public speaking?**

Chapter 7: A Healthy Relationship

Through Communication

Every relationship requires communication. Never is this more important than when you are trying to speak to a loved one, such as a family member or a spouse. To have a healthy relationship requires the ability to express oneself and feel as though you are being heard. It is a give and take situation, but one that can be achieved through hard work and patience.

Tone of Voice

One of the most important things to remember is that the way you say words is often as important as the words you say. When talking to a significant other, remember to treat them with respect and talk to them the way you would like to be talked to. Keep your voice steady and at a quiet volume. When speaking to children, it helps to speak in a very quiet tone so that they will be forced to listen to your actual words and not just your tone. Try to avoid sounding commanding or condescending. This goes both ways; also try not to come across sounding scared or defeated. Remember that your tone will be the first thing heard, well before the actual words so keep it even and you will be assured a good listener.

Think Before You Speak

One of the best pieces of advice ever offered is to think before you speak. If you have something you want to say, review it in your head and be certain of what you are about to say. Change words that may seem too harsh or that have multiple meanings that can be taken out of context. Do your best to speak in simple terms, using smaller words in order to clearly convey your point. It does not do to use large words and show off your intelligence if the person you are speaking to doesn't understand them. Think about your audience before you speak, you should know your significant other pretty well, at least well enough to recognize what words and actions will cause which reactions. Make it a point to avoid those so you can have a nice, effective conversation.

Listen

Communication is not just about speaking, but about listening as well. Open your ears and clear your mind when another is speaking. Do your best to be respectful and show you are listening and that you understand what they are saying. Do not be condescending or patronizing about it, but do try to show interest in what they have to say. Make eye contact and ask questions, supply feedback and speak up if you didn't hear or don't understand something. Communication is not a one-way street.

With as many people as there are on Earth right now, it is almost impossible to get through a day without speaking to anyone. That is why good communication skills are so important. These skills not only affect your home life but also your ability to make friends.

Chapter 8: The Goal That Makes Your Audience Love Your Talk

There is a reason for everything. One big underlying reason.

For anglers, the reason they spend time learning different fishing skills and techniques are for one big reason. The main reason is because they want to be a better angler. This one main reason is the underlying reason why they do everything else.

Athletes spend countless hours doing different forms of training. There is a main reason or goal they have. That is to win their chosen event.

I'm a writer. I spend an awful lot of time learning, researching, testing, and writing. My main goal? To provide the best help and advice I can to as many readers as possible and to make a living out of it.

This is what makes the difference between average speakers and top class ones. When you have a main goal or focus, you will find that everything else you do, will become far easier and much more effective. What's more, your audience will love you. They will love what you say and will hang on your every word.

Many speakers miss this important focus. This is because they get wrapped up in the 'how' and forget about the 'why'. This results in the talk being substandard and not usually remembered. In essence, no benefit to the audience. The most important thing that makes any talk top class, is this one main goal.

But not just any goal. What is it?

Your goal should always be...

To change the lives of your audience for the better.

That is the whole purpose of your talk. To enrich their lives. Make things better than they were before.

This goal should be the foundation of everything you do and say in your talk. You should always be aiming for this outcome. If you have a genuine interest in your audience's welfare, they will see it. This creates trust in what you say.

Remember, you are the one with something they want. Something that will improve their lives.

Here's a good tip.

Imagine your audience were filled with all your friends and family. As long as you get on with your family that is.

By thinking this way, you will naturally be inclined to do your best to help them. Always aim to help your audience in this way.

To summarise

So remember this. Although you will have all these techniques, methods, and tips that make you a better speaker, they should all be used with the intention of changing your audience's lives for the better. That should always be your main goal.

Chapter 9: Know The Best Presentation Structure

Step #9 Confirm your presentation include the 3 pillars.

There are three pillars for the presentation and they are equally weighted:

Content: Proper content should be presents (not time waste).

Structure: Good structure as described in this chapter.

Delivery: Audience interaction and feedback (in Chapter 4)

You should confirm that your presentation include the three pillars.

Step #10 Make structure for your presentation.

You should make the structure of your presentation because presentation is like a flight:

It should have a beginning (Flight takeoff), It should have a middle (normal flying duration) and it should have an ending (Flight landing).

Imagine a flight which took off well and all the flying duration it was good. At the end the landing was very bad.

Would the passengers say it was a good flight?? Of course no, they will regret to ride a flight with this airways company.

The presentation structure should be as follows:

Beginning: It is the introduction for your presentation. You should make "**Opening**" to immediately attract the attention and the interest from your audience.

Middle: It is the main body and the core content of your presentation. You should state and mention clearly the message of the presentation and the "**Evidence**".

End: The conclusion and the final message. You should leave the audience with memorable "**Closing**".

We will explain each one individually:

The Opening

There are different opening methods:

Question on a need:

You can start saying "**If I could tell you a program that will make you loose 20 pounds in a single month, you sure want to listen, wouldn't you?**". This could be applied if you are giving a presentation about new nutrition system to fat people.

Study the needs and wants of your audience.

Startling statement:

You can start with information like "**Last year United Nations spent over I billion dollars on poverty in Africa.**" this could be good startling statement that captures audience attention.

Compliment statement:

You can start with "Your chairman told me that you are the best engineers in the company and you are the company future.

So I hope I will add a value to you through this course"

This will grab their interest and turn on their ambition.

Dramatic incident:

You can start with dramatic story that will capture the audience attention and make them focus with you.

The story should be compatible with the presentation subject not away from the presentation purpose.

The middle

The middle of the presentation should include credibility and evidence to stick the message in the audience minds.

Any evidence should DEFAT doubts.

D E F E A T S

- **D**emonstration
- **E**xhibit
- **F**act
- **E**xample
- **A**nalogy
- **T**estimonial
- **S**tatistics

The used evidence should be one of the above mentioned terminologies.

Demonstration: You show to your audience that something already works.

Example: Show the audience real experience occurred.

Fact: Things specific and proven (taken for granted).

Exhibits: Picture or model or a map.

Analogy: compare with other cases.

Testimonial: quote of an authorized person.

Statistics: Trends, graphs or percentages.

Always support your middle structure with evidence.

The closing

This is the end of the presentation, it should be presented in a right way to stick and last in the audience minds.

Also there are different closing methods:

Summarize the presentation in few words:

You can say "At the end of our presentation we conclude the following keywords …..".

Mention the benefit from the presentation:

You can say "This will be better for our society" **or** "For our country".

Apply a challenge:

You can say "It is now up to you, can you do it?"

Use final view:

You can use one slide to show what the final picture would look like in the future.

Step #11 Use the 4 (P)s model for your presentation.

The four Ps is PLAN, PREPARE, PRACTICE, PRESENTATION.

PLAN

Firstly you plan your presentation by mind mapping, brain storming and comparing your information with benchmarking.

Good planning will make you open to opportunities and allow you to overcome fears inside you.

PREPARE

Prepare your presentation with the following strategy:

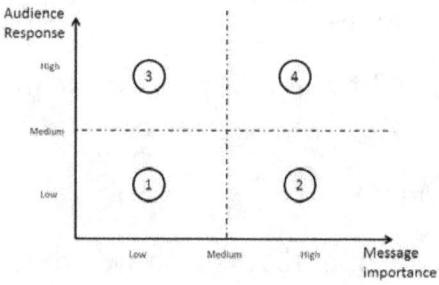

Strategy #1:

If your presentation topic is a low importance message (like entertainment shows, stand up comedy ...etc.), so you should consider a low audience response.

Strategy #2:

If your presentation topic is a high importance message (like teaching), so you give an effort to convey the message and you might find a low audience response because your audience has no experience about the topic you are teaching.

Strategy #3:

If your presentation topic is a low importance message for your audience (like you try to convince people of something using evidence), so you should perform in a way that you would expect a high audience response for your proofs.

Strategy #4:

If your presentation topic is a high importance message for you (like sales persons) or you are trying to take a bank loan, So you should perform in a way that you would expect a high audience response and call them to take action (using phrases like "what's next" or "buy now") to encourage them to take the action.

This strategy will pass all the previous three strategies.

The 4Ps model information flow is as follows:

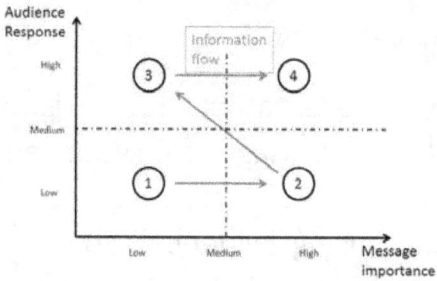

To apply the strategy#2, you will pass with strategy#1.

It means if you are teaching your audience you will consider low audience response and low message importance at the beginning, then you will change the low message importance (relative to your audience) from low to high(ex: like showing that when you understand the lesson you will pass the next exam).

To apply the strategy#4, you will pass with strategy#1,2,&3.

It means that when you want to make a product sale for example new Samsung tablet:

You will not tell your audience directly "buy the product"!!

You will start with the strategy #1 with some entertaining and humor to attract the audience, then strategy #2 showing the audience the importance of the message (the new tablet features and capability), then direct the show to audience interaction trying to get their high response and questions, then direct them to purchasing with a call of action (like what you are waiting for? Buy now!!), or use the magic formula.

Step #12 Use the magic formula.

When your presentation is about a "call to action" use this magic formula:

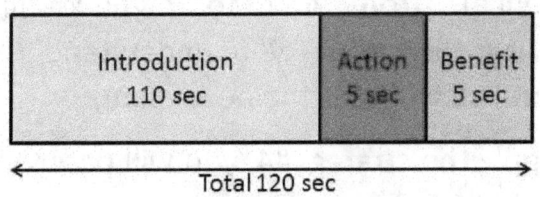

The magic formula starts with about 110 seconds introduction about the subject, then 5 seconds calling for action followed by another 5 seconds stating the benefit from the action.

Example:

You are giving a sales public speech to old people in India. You are trying to convince them to buy your company cellphones.

You can use the magic formula as follows:

"While my friend's father was on a vacation in Morocco last summer, he was in a safari trip by 4x4 Jeep car. He had an accident that the car was broke down and will not work again. He was with his friend and his friend didn't own a cell phone. If my friend's father didn't take his cell phone with him, he and his friend will get lost and they will not survive".

(End of the introduction 110 sec)

So, buy a cell phone now!!

(Call of action 5 sec)

And you will not get lost anywhere and will be safe.

(Stating the benefit 5 sec)

The magic formula is a proven way for convincing audience and "Calling for action" method.

Chapter 10: How Public Speaking Can Help Your Career

Public speaking is a great way of building personal development on many levels, since improving communication skills is helpful in almost every area of life. Whether your goal is to engage in political debate, make a career as a motivational speaker or gain confidence in front of an audience, public speaking can help you meet your goal. Below are some of the benefits you can get by speaking in Public

1. Boost confidence and Self-Esteem

Public speaking can significantly boost your confidence. Overcoming the fears and insecurities that accompany public speaking is empowering. Furthermore, connecting with audiences can be a strong reminder that you have valuable insights and opinions to share with the world.

Your confidence levels will grow as you go from speaking to small groups of people up to large audiences..

2.Improve communication skills

When you write a speech, you have to think carefully about the best framework, persuasive strategy, and diction to communicate your message to the audience. This type of thinking can help you improve your communication skills in other areas of your life.

Personal relationships, social interactions, and work situations require you to communicate ideas to other people. Public speaking focuses on communicating ideas. You can learn to calmly take up an opposing view, to present your ideas in an organized and coherent manner, and to defend your views to others.

3.Expand your professional network

Another benefit of public speaking is that when you speak at an event, you will suddenly find that everyone wants to talk with you. This is a valuable opportunity for making friends, building business contacts and generating business.

Not only this, but you also get the opportunity to network with other speakers, some of whom may be very difficult to contact normally. Speaking events may also have guest rooms for speakers where they are given food and drink and can network together.

4.Helps you drive change

Who do we listen to more, someone talking to us in person or an email? The person speaking is always going to be more convincing than a note sent across the internet. You could spend your time going from person to person if that's your comfort zone.

But think about how many more people you could reach if you stood up on stage and had them all gathered together in an audience. The more people you're able to speak to, the more change you can implement.

Developed your listening, reading and writing skills

Preparing effective speeches involves considering your audience which means listening carefully and sensitively to what they're saying. You'll also hone your reading through research, and your writing through wanting to communicate effectively

Increased your social network considerable

Putting yourself forward makes it easier for you to meet others. You'll find people want to talk to you - your spirit of "can-do" is attractive, energizing. You will draw people to you.

Chapter 11: Talking With Anyone – What Do You Need?

Summary

There are only a few things you need to know in order to speak effectively with just about anyone. The most important of them, of course, is confidence.

Talking with Anyone – What Do You Need?

If you are the type that sits alone at a party with a hundred people just because you don't know anyone there, you definitely need to improve your skills of communication. Communication is the key to anything – making friendships, striking business contracts, impressing people and even getting yourself a life partner. You cannot do any of these without talking with someone.

But if talking with someone unfamiliar is something that scares the heebie-jeebies out of you, you need a quick sizing up.

Probably something is seriously wrong there. Talking is actually one of the natural things that we do – it is as natural as breathing for most of us – so what's holding you back.

Let us begin by trying to see the most important things that you will need in order to be able to talk with anyone.

Note that I will always use the phrase "talking with someone' here as opposed to "talking to someone'. This is not about grammar, but it is more about what I think. Talking is not something you do alone. You do it with someone. It is not that you just keep on going blah-blah and the other person just listens. They are talking with you too. It is a collaborated effort.

Confidence

The first thing you need to start any kind of conversation is confidence. Here confidence basically means that you should have some knowledge of your self-worth. You should know that you amount to something and that is what you need to project when you are trying to open a conversation with someone. It is only when they understand that listening to you will mean something to them will they take the time. However, your confidence will only show when you are really happy with your self-worth. Hence, this is more about a self-evolvement thing than personality development.

Be Considerate

I would say this is what gives the power to keep any conversation going. What does being considerate mean in this context? It simply means this – You have to be as much aware of the other person as you are about yourself. If you get a break at a conversation with someone, it does not mean that you will just go on rambling about yourself. Give an equal opportunity to the other to speak. Listen to what they say. Ask about them. Make them feel important in the talk too.

Be Diverse

You may start with a single topic, but if you want to keep a conversation going on, it is best to be diverse. Once you know what the person likes, you could continue talking about that subject. But it would be foolish to talk about Hollywood thrillers to a person who hasn't ever watched a movie, wouldn't it? You must make an effort to keep broadening your vistas of knowledge all the time. Remember that the more you know the more will you be able to talk.

Remember

A conversation commits partial suicide when you forget an important detail about someone. It would be ridiculous if you have been speaking with someone for fifteen minutes and you have already forgotten their name which they mentioned. On the other hand, if you speak specifically to someone about something that pertains to them, you will almost always get a good reply. A good memory is vital to good conversation; I have always experienced that.

Chapter 12: Boot Camp: Preparing Yourself

Athletes train for years before participating in competitions to make sure that they are in the best form and increase their chances of winning. Nineteen year old Olympic Gold Medalist Gymnast Simone Biles started training at 8 years old. She spent hours practicing and had to nurse multiple injuries in her quest to become successful. You will also need to invest time and effort in your journey to becoming a successful and efficient speaker. Preparation is certainly the key to having a better experience at public speaking.

Preparing yourself involves more than just researching and writing what you are going to say. You will need to prepare both physically and mentally for the event. Below are some tips you can use to become an effective speaker:

Unmasking Your Monster

People often refer to something they are scared of as monsters. Public speaking is a monster for some people. If you feel anxious about being asked to speak in front of others then it to may be your monster.

Monsters of course are meant to be beaten and of course, you can certainly beat your monster. In order to do so, you need to look beyond the fear and be clinically methodical. You need to be objective as to how you perceive public speaking.

Create a list of why you feel anxious about speaking in front of an audience. This can include items such as the examples below:

I might get booed

People may get bored and walk out

I do not know what to say

What if I trip and fall

I am naturally shy

I do not like people staring at me

What if my slideshow presentations do not work

Where do I look

How do I start

By creating a list you quantify what you are afraid of, thus making it easier to understand. You can then start addressing each item individually if needed. In addition, by seeing the reasons behind your fear, you will be able to identify a starting point on how you can overcome it.

For example, in the list given above, being naturally shy can certainly make you anxious about being in the spotlight. You can start by slowly overcoming your shyness in small steps like starting conversations with co-workers or friends. If one of your reasons is you are afraid of tripping or falling, then you can make sure that you wear comfortable shoes and clothing to prevent this from happening.

The list gives you power over your monster. The more specific your reasons become, the easier it is to find the solutions. And once you see that it is a situation that you have control over, you will start feeling less anxious.

Having a list also helps you realize which of the reasons are valid and which ones you are simply using as cop-outs. By coming up with the solutions, you take the most important first step towards overcoming your fear.

Hone Your Skills

Whether you are a seasoned speaker or a first timer, preparation is still crucial. One of the best ways to do it is to hone your skills. If you are comfortable with prepared speeches, then pump up your arsenal by practicing how to do impromptu ones. You can work on organizing your thoughts to be able to deliver logical and engaging speeches or toasts.

Some of the things you can work on include the following:

Grammar – This is the foundation of every successful speech. You want your audience to be captivated and engaged. It would be difficult to manage this if you are unable to fully express your ideas in the right way. Grammatical errors can affect the message you want to relay and confuse your listeners. Using incorrect prepositions and grammar structures have a huge impact. Sadly, being a native speaker of your language does not always guaranty that you are an expert on semantics. Reviewing grammar rules can be a big help. There are numerous online resources that you can use to help you out with this.

Vocabulary – When you are talking to a specific audience, repeating words over and over can become exhausting both to you and your listener. By enriching your vocabulary, you can find synonyms or other ways to express your idea without using the same words. You can also simplify concepts that your audience might find a little complicated. For example, if you are giving a speech on selling techniques, you can refer to the customers as consumers or buyers as well.

Subject Knowledge – If you are a resource speaker for a specific subject or topic, then it would be beneficial to ensure that you are consistently well versed on your area of expertise. Stay up to date with developments in your field.

Enunciation – You want to make sure that your audience fully understands your message. Speaking clearly helps you achieve this. Listeners tend to get restless and bored when they have difficulty understanding what the speaker is saying.

Choreography – Standing stiff in front of a crowd may be uncomfortable both to you and to your listeners. Even if you had a podium to use, you will need to incorporate some movement into your speech. This makes you appear more open and easier to identify with. Different elements to enhance your stage presence will be discussed further in later chapters of this book.

The Next Step

If you regularly do speeches, you can still benefit from proper preparation. Take time to evaluate your previous performance so you identify ways to improve yourself.

Avoid focusing on your errors as this would have a negative impact on your morale and confidence. While these are still important to take note of, there is no need to give yourself a hard time on what can no longer be changed.

Make a list of the highlights of your previous speech and a brief description of how it made the experience a success. This will help you create a habit so it becomes a standard in all your public speaking events.

You can also make a list of what you wish to improve on. These could be elements such as how you move around the stage or how you segue from one idea to another.

Practice – Rehearsing your prepared speech can go a long way. But most speakers tend to practice only when they have an upcoming speaking engagement. Regular practice with or without a scheduled speech will help you improve your techniques. You can use speeches that you have previously delivered as material for your practice sessions. Here are some ways through which you can enhance your skills:

Practicing in Front of a Mirror – Your facial expressions have a huge impact on how your audience will react to your statements. It establishes your credibility along with your other body language. While you think you may have it under control, there are times when your expressions may change subconsciously. Practicing in front of a mirror will increase your awareness of these instances. You might be surprised at some of your reactions as you are usually unaware that these are happening as you speak.

Another benefit to practicing in front of the mirror is that you will be able to work on how to make eye contact. It can be a bit disorienting to look into someone else's eyes. Not being ready may disrupt your train of thought. By getting used to looking into your own eyes first, you can gradually ease into looking into others.

Record Yourself – Once you have become comfortable with practicing in front of the mirror, the next step is to record yourself while you are delivering your speech. This will help you evaluate yourself from an audience's point of view. From a different vantage, you can assess your choreography, body language, and delivery. You can record different practices so you can monitor your improvement as well.

Practice with an Audience – You can ask your friends or family members to help you out with this part of your preparation. While their feedback will be priceless, you can also use this opportunity to become more comfortable being in front of an actual live audience.

Practicing on your own may help you enhance your skills but having listeners may be a bit disconcerting. When you practice with an audience, you can work on how you can manage being nervous and how to interact with them. Eye contact, proper pausing, and an active communication with your listeners are just some of the elements you can enhance with this type of practice.

If you feel that your friends or loved ones might not give you an honest review, you can invite at least 2 people. Provide them with an evaluation sheet that they can check or fill out so they have an idea of what elements of your performance they need to focus on.

Practice and preparation are by no means overrated. By preparing yourself before an actual speaking engagement, you will be able to reduce your anxiety if you have stage fright. If you are already comfortable giving speeches, ample preparation can enhance the experience for both you and your listeners.

Chapter 13: How To Structure Your Speech

Structure

Speech structures can vary from those that are downright utilitarian (no nonsense, hyper-logical, gets the job done) to those that have a little more creativity and artistic flair.

In this chapter, you'll learn the basic template that virtually all speeches should follow, all the ins and outs of different sections of your speech, as well as ways you can make your speech highly unique and add your own creative touch to make for an unforgettable speech.

Read on to learn how to structure your speech for maximum impact...

The First 30 Seconds: The Most Important Part of Your Speech

The first thirty seconds (or in many cases, even less) of your speech are the most important. What you say during these crucial first moments will determine whether your listeners seat themselves on the edge of their seats, eager to hear what you have to say next, or zone out and wait for you to finish without really listening to what you have to say.

So... how can you get your audience engaged from the get-go? Here are some different ways you can do just that...

Attention Grabbers

Immediately grab your audience's attention and capture their interest with one of the following:

- Ask a thought-provoking question.

- Tell a story or anecdote.

- Make a startling statement or reveal an astonishing fact.

- Icebreaker—make a joke (risky as this may backfire) or a reference to the audience, occasion, previous speech, current events (especially within your industry), etc.

- Relevant quotation (and if you like to be bold, perhaps one that is controversial or shocking).

- Expert opinion or prediction (be careful with predictions though because if your prediction turns out to be wrong, this will hurt your credibility in the future).

- And more, so get creative. The "attention grabber" you use to open your speech may also depend on the purpose of your speech, who your audience is, or your industry. For a creative example, read on below…

A brilliant example of an attention grabber is from Dan Pink's TED talk: "The Puzzle of Motivation." (See the TED talk here: https://www.ted.com/talks/dan_pink_on_motivation/). He starts off his speech by saying the following:

"I need to make a confession at the outset here. A little over 20 years ago, I did something that I regret, something that I'm not particularly proud of. Something that, in many ways, I wish no one would ever know, but here I feel kind of obliged to reveal. (Audience laughter.) In the late 1980s, in a moment of youthful indiscretion, I went to law school. (Audience laughter.)"

Now, I don't know about you, but that sure grabbed my attention and got me eager to hear what he had to say next.

Moving on, let's now take a look at something else that can be important when starting a speech and making a good first impression with your audience…

SEE Factors

In direct marketing (e.g. door-to-door sales), you're taught to do two major things when you first start talking to someone you're pitching: icebreakers and SEE factors.

You break the ice by making a relevant joke, mentioning something about the surroundings, or just saying g'day and asking them how their day is.

Whereas breaking the ice has more to do with what you actually say, SEE factors have more to do with your nonverbal communication. "SEE" is an acronym: **s**mile, **e**ye contact, **e**xcitement (or **e**nthusiasm—after all, you don't want to look unenthusiastic about what you're selling).

While SEE factors is something taught in sales, it can also be applied to public speaking. Within those crucial first thirty seconds, you want to:

- **Smile.** Or at least look happy to be there, you don't necessarily need to grin like a fool. (Note: It is still important to be aware of your situation. For example, if you're giving a eulogy, it might not be very appropriate to give everyone a big grin.)

- **Make eye contact.** At the beginning of your speech, before you start, you can scan the audience. As you speak, you'll want to keep your eyes on the audience. Don't look at your feet, your notes, at the PowerPoint slide, or anything else. No.

Always look at the audience. If you're concerned about being distracted by people's faces, look slightly above people's heads or look at the back of the room.

- **Show excitement and enthusiasm.** If you don't care about what you've got to say, why should anybody else? Don't talk like a boring old university professor who's giving the same lecture for the 40th year in a row and boring his students brainless. Instead, speak with passion and vigor. (Once again, you need to be aware of your situation. Continuing the eulogy example, you'll want to show that you care about what you have to say not with excitement and enthusiasm, but perhaps with solemness and admiration for the deceased's accomplishments, the way they lived their life, and those whose lives they've touched, etc.)

Your first thirty seconds are crucial. Within those thirty seconds (or less), you must grab your audience's attention, get them interested in what you have to say, and then make a smooth if not seamless transition into the rest of your speech.

Now that you've grabbed your audience's attention and made a favorable impression by smiling, making eye contact, and showing enthusiasm for what you're going to be talking to them about, let's take a look at what you should do next…

Tell Them What You're Going to Tell Them: How to Introduce What You're Talking About in a Unique and Engaging Way

"Almost every guidebook for speech writing will say to choose your topic. It's an obvious starting place. But a lot of people miss out the fact that you need to also select the core message that you want to get across."

— Ryan McLean

Once you've deployed your attention grabber, you'll need to introduce the topic you're going to talk about (i.e. "tell them what you're going to tell them"). Ideally, you will incorporate this into your "attention grabber" in your first thirty seconds.

For example, if you're giving a talk about self-driving cars, you might start by telling a story about a friend of yours who was killed in a car accident when you were younger. You can then link this into what your speech will be about by telling the audience that this tragic event inspired you to want create a world in which what happened to your friend would not have happened through your work in the development of self-driving cars. Then, having got the audience's attention, you can then introduce what your speech is about by briefly outlining three reasons self-driving cars will make roads safer (or whatever the main points are that you will make in your speech).

Here is a brief, step-by-step guide for starting your speech in a powerful way:

Pause. Don't immediately start talking. Take a few moments to take a breath, scan the audience, and relax. This will get all eyes on you as well as give you an aura of confidence and power. Then, once your silence has got everybody's attention and all eyes are on you…

Deploy your attention grabber. Start with a story, controversial statement, a relevant quote, anecdote, etc. See above for a whole list of different attention grabbers. Make sure to relate your attention grabber to the topic of your speech and then…

State the purpose of your speech. Why should your audience care? How does it relate to them? Why are you speaking? What are you trying to accomplish with this speech? Let your audience know the purpose of your speech. Make them want to listen. State your purpose very concisely with a single sentence. Don't waffle on. Then…

Tell them what you're going to tell them. What will your main points be? Succinctly state what you're going to tell them. For example, if you have three major points that you're going to expound upon in your speech, briefly state them.

Now remember, you need to do all of this quickly (though don't speak quickly). Be concise. You want your introduction to feel more like a surgeon's scalpel than a rusty axe.

It's simple:

Grab their attention with a quote, controversial statement, short story, or other attention grabber.

Tell them why you're there.

Tell them what you're going to tell them.

That's it. It should take no more than 30 seconds (unless you're giving a long speech).

Ken Robinson's TED talk: "Do Schools Kill Creativity?" gives us a great example of a solid introduction (See the TED talk here: http://www.ted.com/talks/ken_robinson_says_schools_kill_creativity/).

It's very simple, yet gets the job done.

Robinson **breaks the ice** by starting his speech in a very conversational way and getting a few laughs.

"Good morning. How are you? (Audience laughter.) It's been great, hasn't it? I've been blown away by the whole thing. In fact, I'm leaving. (Audience laughter.)"

He then **outlines the three main points** he is going to talk about.

"There have been three themes running through the conference which are relevant to what I want to talk about. One is the [...]. The second is that [...]. And the third part is that [...]."

He then finishes up his introduction by concisely **stating the purpose of his speech.**

"So I want to talk about education and I want to talk about creativity. My contention is that creativity now is as important in education as literacy, and we should treat it with the same status. (Audience applause.)"

It's really that simple.

Body: Tell Them

So you've grabbed their attention, told them what you're going to tell them by briefly outlining your main points, and you've told them the purpose of your speech.

Now what?

Now you just need to tell them.

Ask yourself: what is the purpose of your speech? What are you trying to do? Are you trying to convince? Persuade? Educate? Inspire action?

The way you structure your speech will depend a great deal on what it is you're trying to accomplish (i.e. the purpose of your speech).

That said, regardless of what you're discussing or what you're trying to accomplish, the body/middle of your speech will almost always need the following two things:

The body of your speech will need to be organized around a few key points or main ideas. You need structure. You can't just toss out random idea after random idea and try to bumble together a string of random thoughts. Limit your speech to three main ideas (or "key points", or "arguments", or whatever you want to call them). If your speech is a little on the longer side, you may be able to get away with five main ideas.

The body of your speech will need signposting and transitions. You need to make it abundantly clear that you're discussing your first point, or your second, or so on by signposting. Give your audience a helping hand and remind them of where they are in the speech. For example, you will want to say things like, "My first point is [X]," and "Moving on to my second point..." You will also need smooth transitions so your speech doesn't feel too clunky. Smooth it out with transitions that express relationships between the points you're making.

As for how to structure each of your main points, ideas, or arguments, here is a basic template to follow. It goes by the acronym "PEEL" (you can think of it as a way to "peel" away the different layers of an idea you're discussing or a point you are making). Here it is:

Point. State your point/idea/argument concisely in one sentence. A good example comes from Amy Cuddy's TED talk: "Your Body Language Shapes Who You Are" (See the TED talk here: http://www.ted.com/talks/amy_cuddy_your_body_language_shapes_who_you_are/). When she starts discussing her second main idea, she says this (notice also that she signposts): "So the second question really was, you know, so we know that our minds change our bodies, but is it also true that our bodies change our minds?" That's it.

Elaborate. Obviously, a single sentence isn't enough to fully explore one of your main points. So dedicate another sentence (or two, or three) to delving into this point on a deeper level. You can mention or discuss any supporting ideas or subtopics—ideas that support your main point(s).

Evidence. Now you need to support your claim or point with evidence. This is where you bring up examples, facts, figures, statistics, stories, and any other evidence you want to share with your audience.

Link. Summarize your point, demonstrate that it supports your main idea and/or the purpose of your speech. Then, for a smooth transition, "link" it to the next point or idea you are going to discuss.

Now reading that structure probably makes you a little... bored. I'll be the first to admit it's not the most exciting thing in the world. However, it's just that: a structure. Here's how to make it a little more exciting and make sure your audience remembers what you've told them...

The Secret to Being Impossible to Forget

If you've listened to many speeches, there's probably a fair chunk of them where you can't remember a single thing they told you. You don't want this to be you. So here's how to ensure you make your message and points unforgettable...

The first key to having your audience remember what you've told them is to understand how people actually remember things. There are four stages:

Hearing. First, your audience must hear what it is you have to say. They're not going to remember it if they couldn't hear you.

Attention. Second, you must have their attention. We can only consciously focus on one thing at a time. If they're on their phone or daydreaming about their next vacation, they're not going to remember what you said.

Understanding. Third, they must understand what you're telling them. In high school, I **heard** my chemistry teacher speak. He even had my full **attention**. But I didn't understand most of it. So I didn't remember it. Simple enough.

Remembering. Finally, if your audience can hear you and you've got their attention and they understand the points you are making, they will be able to remember it. You can also help them remember your points with the techniques below...

Read below for some different ways you can grab your audience's attention, help them to understand a point you're making, and, of course, remember...

- **Humor.** Humor hits several birds with one stone. Humor grabs your audience's attention. Humor is memorable. And humor can also help your audience understand a point you're making.

- **Relevance.** How is what you're saying relevant to them? How can they apply it to their own life? How does what you're saying affect them?

- **Examples.** Examples help make your message easier to grasp.

- **Stories.** Us humans are hardwired to remember stories much, much, **much** better than standalone facts. Use this to your advantage by doing a bit of storytelling.

- **Visuals.** Do **not** make the mistake of using your PowerPoint as a crutch. It is not there for you to read off. It is not there for your audience to read off, either (they should be listening to you instead). Ideally, your presentation slides should either have only a few words (e.g. a **very** concise statement—your main point) or graphics (and they should likewise be very simple graphics, not distracting ones). Just look at a Steve Jobs presentation to see what I mean. Anyway, visuals—if used right—can definitely help your audience to remember and understand what you're saying. They can also help you retain everybody's attention.

- **Contrast.** "To be or not to be?" "Float like a butterfly, sting like a bee." "The best means of insuring peace is to be prepared for war." Compare and contrast your ideas. Contrast does a great job of yanking our attention. It also makes things very easy to understand, helping us to remember.

- **Repetition.** Repetition makes things much easier to remember. Martin Luther King's "I Have a Dream" speech is a great example of this. King repeated "I have a dream..." eight times in a row, expressing different ideas, hopes, and dreams. Obama is also a big fan of repetition. For example, during his 2004 keynote speech at the Democratic National Convention, Obama repeated many times, "There's not an [X] America and a [Y] America; there's a United States of America."

Moving on, let's take a look at how to finish your speech with impact and leave your audience wowed...

Conclusion: Tell Them What You Told Them

You've given your speech. You seized your audience's attention from the get-go with a powerful introduction. You then discussed your main points in an engaging and interesting way, winning your audience over to your way of thinking.

Now what?

Now you need to finish your speech off with a bang. You need to end on a high note. Here's a basic template for finishing your speech:

Restate your purpose. Reiterate the message, lesson, or key things that you want your audience to remember.

Summarize your main points. Briefly restate each of your three (or however many) main points. In other words, "tell 'em what you told 'em."

Your final statement. Finish off with a broader statement, showing your audience how what you've told them relates to the big picture. You can also finish by referring back to your attention grabber at the very beginning of your speech. For example, remember how, in his TED talk, Dan Pink started off by "confessing" that he went to law school?

Well, here's how he finished his speech: "I rest my case." You can finish off your speech in a similar fashion by going back to your initial attention grabber.

It's really that simple.

Restate the one big thing you want your audience to remember (the purpose of your speech).

Summarize your main points.

Return to your opening theme/attention grabber.

Done.

Chapter 14: The Power Of Examples In Public Speaking

Offering examples through your speaking presentation is one of the most crucial and critical strategies to refining your public speaking technique. Great examples are important in captivating the listeners and showing that you are knowledgeable of your content.

Examples benefit the listener in several distinctive locations. First off, good examples help to promote your main point. Illustrations enable the listener to comprehend the primary element — furthermore, good examples guide the audience to recollect the top topics later.

Good examples can be a excellent approach to support and validate the primary remarks you make. All through your demonstration, you are going to be making various arguments of fact and judgment. Both of those may very well be complemented by showing good examples and illustrations. These provide you with an alternate point of view to the case. An assertion of fact may be validated with factual data — a declaration of belief is usually backed with authentic life demonstrations or citings. While a listener has just your own promise to go on without having an example, good illustrations provide additional backing for the subject matter.

Illustrations tend to be the perfect method for the crowd to understand the subject matter. Consider that you are a expert on what you are presenting on. Probably you will have been in the topic for many years, or maybe you have a unique and strong history in it. Or possibly, you happen to be a resident pro in the details. Either way, there is an excellent likelihood your demonstration is going to have attributes that happen to be hard for the average listener to comprehend. A powerful illustration, preferably a real life example that every attendee can connect with, will make it easy for the crowd to digest your subject matter. Good examples really are a presentation's wonderful equalizer: they provide context to just about every statement.

And lastly, good illustrations help out the attendee to remember and retain. With subject matter that's sophisticated and multi-faceted, any attendee may have a problematic time recollecting and remembering that which was presented. Considering that the objective of a presentation is nearly always training, remembrance is quite critical. Communication skills training educates the presenter to make an effort to help the audience by providing them with beneficial knowledge. Great examples permit the audience to have a memory device to attach to the topic. A listener is much more inclined to not forget an instance or account, rather than the key point. Even so, the case gives the attendee the context to recollect the general subject matter.

Precisely what is a good illustration? For starters, a good illustration is one which is appropriate for the bulk of the audience. Complete your homework, and be aware of the demographics of the listeners. Plan your illustrations ahead of time and be certain that they are pertinent. Always focus your examples on generalities, and not on specifics. The more your example refers to a standard idea, the better likelihood it holds to get considered. And then, your illustration needs to be convincing. Even though your subject matter could possibly be regarded as by many to be esoteric and enigmatic, a real example will allow the viewers to remain engaged and center on the data.

Also, make sure that the illustration always compliments your speech. It is important to put this into practice in each and every public presentation. An audience will stay engaged, and keep hold of a substantial quantity of information if you provide quality illustrations.

USING VOICE INFLECTION IN PUBLIC SPEAKING

Voice Inflection, or the style by which we apply our voice through tone, pitch, and speed, has a big impact in the overall delivery of a public speech. Voice inflection may be used as a tool to help you carry a point, elevate awareness, or focus the audience. After the business presenter is familiar with the particulars regarding utilizing voice inflection, it is easy to implement them in their following speaking discussion.

In realistic terms, voice inflection carries numerous levels of importance within a business discussion. To start, inflection has to do with the pitch you deliver the speech. The higher tones, along with the lower tones, and the frequency that you bounce back and forth amongst the two. Likewise, inflection has to do with the speed of presentation of the content. Plenty of speakers offer their info fast, even while other presenters deliver slowly, and still some others go back and forth.

The pitch of voice will allow the crowd to put more or less focus on various words from your discussion. Not every phrase you mention can be of identical significance, and this social norm is a structure from where the significance of voice inflection exists. Pitch, plus the wide variety of pitch, focuses the audience to the critical components and vital details of one's speech. Start using a elevated pitch to relay enthusiasm with regards to a topic or critical point. Use a lower pitch to imply seriousness and reverence regarding a topic matter. Most of all, vary the pitch throughout the speech. In the case that you do not alter your pitch, you inescapably give every single word and every sentence the same value. Public speaking skills requires you to direct your audience. To do this effectively, you must be able to use the pitch within your voice as one of the preferred means.

The pace of delivery of a business presentation models the tone and momentum for your audience. Speed, or absence thereof, allows the public speaker to show meaning, depth, and importance. Once again, going in between speeds may be the most critical aspect. Speeding through an example helps you to build up enthusiasm. Often times, a speaker will use synonyms and anecdotes, while presenting rather quickly, to offer a poignant and conclusive bit of material. Slowing down for a portion of the message acts to set serious emphasis, and pushes a point home. Even more so, the influence of the pause, provided right after a vital point, has been verified to allow the listeners to hold on to the material noticeably better.

In addition to that, there are various other details that only add more to the benefits of your inflection. De-stress your voice while you deliver at the front of a large audience. Even while this may look tough to do in the beginning, try practicing the variations in talking with a calm throat and neck, rather than when the throat and neck are stiffened. Calming the muscular tissues all-around your throat will relax your voice. A calm voice sounds considerably better and more pleasing to your listeners. Likewise, articulate your words and phrases and enunciate. Public speakers have a tendency to rush fairly quickly through their content material, which can entail mumbling through the individual words that comprise the sentences. Very clear articulation can help your attendee to clearly comprehend every little thing you're attempting to say. A tranquil voice and clear articulation compliment correct voice inflection.

Voice inflection is an important component of public speaking. Inflection possesses the ability to bring your listeners in and out of a variety of points, and lock in certain important takeaways. Additionally, it keeps the audience interested and receptive. This is an impressive technique in perfecting the art of public speaking.

Chapter 15: Fear Of Public Speaking

The greats once felt fear

I will try to keep this chapter short because there is not much to it when it comes to fear at the end of the day you are either willing to act in spite of fear or you aren't. If you feel fear when speaking in public and it freezes you up when standing in front of an audience, then you'll need to develop the why! Why do you want to improve your public speaking skills, why are you willing to go through this fear and present what you have to offer, do you believe your voice is worth listening to? Guess what people who are successful & considered experts in their field of practice have an inner confidence when it comes to public speaking and believe in their selves to deliver value to an audience. They believe what they have to say matters and that others listening will not just care as well but take the information to heart. When you listen to someone who gave a great speech do you believe that person was always good at it? Do you think they were always fearless and had the ability to electrify, inspire and captivate an audience? Well if you haven't guessed it already this wasn't always the case, for anyone who now speaks in public. Look at some of the masters Les Brown once upon a time he was nearly labelled mentally retarded while at school, he wasn't expected to go far in life. Now he is considered one of the top motivational speakers in the world and he had to overcome the fear of public speaking as well. These people we see doing great things are not superstars themselves but just ordinary people like us doing unordinary things. President Obama, Nelson Mandela just to name a few all had to deal with the fear of public speaking at some point in their lives. Now these people will be remembered for the rest of history. If they had let the fear paralyse them in pursuing their dreams, then they would not have done what they have done.

Why is it best to feel the fear?

So why do you feel fear? Well, fear is not a bad thing you are supposed to feel fear. Hundreds of generations ago human civilisation was about survival when you felt fear then it was to help protect you from death. That's really what the mind is a survival mechanism as T. Harv Ecker once said. It is there to keep you safe and alive. However today this survival mechanism we have in our head no longer serves us in practical day to day living. When you break apart the letters that spell fear you have the analogy "FALSE EVIDENCE APPEARING REAL". That is really all fear is false evidence. So when would feel this? The most prevalent time for me is just before a speech or during the first few minutes. That's the time it's heightened the most and greatest in intensity. Towards the end of a speech and especially just after I finish I feel an enormous amount of wellbeing and confidence rush over me. Crazy to believe that 10 minutes earlier my heart was beating really fast and I was fully feeling the fear of presenting, but once I took action got up and spoke in front of an audience the fear almost disappeared instantly after I completed the speech. Now you could say this is because I went back to my comfort zone but at this point I am still feeling the adrenalin rush, the only difference at the end was I felt confidence not fear and even the slight drive to go back on stage and speak again. This, of course, isn't a coincidence it's because I took action presented and felt the fear anyway and that is why I felt good about myself afterwards. In other cases, where I've had the opportunity to speak in public but not take it the fear still came up but as soon as the opportunity passed the fear subsided again. Just, this time, I felt bad about myself for not taking the chance to speak and every time I let those moments pass by I instantly regret it. Is this how you feel? Is this the problem you face when it comes to making a speech? Preparation & practise are what separates a good speech from a great speech and by doing this it will surely help reduce the fear you feel but the main remedy to conquering fear is to spend more time speaking in front of people. In other words, you have to face what you fear most no exceptions. The more you get up on stage and talk to an audience eventually the more comfortable you'll become with the process. Bit by bit the fear will go away the more comfortable you get speaking on stage. Don't worry about how long this may take it's never the same for everyone, for some it will naturally take longer for others they'll pick it up faster. Don't spend any time analysing why this is there are a hundred different reasons why this may be the case, naming a few right now that person could be an extrovert, they may have a job or hobby that requires communication and engagement. Other reasons could be they have a large social circle and find speaking just comes easily and naturally to them. Whatever the reason it doesn't matter all that matters is that you continue and get up and speak. It may help to just not compare yourself to other people and instead compare yourself to where you use to be.

The fear will never go away

The truth is you'll never conquer fear even if you master public speaking the fear will not go away permanently. Why is this? Well for example if you practise public speaking for a year and remove your fear of speaking in public it can still come back, say if you take a break for a month from it and then return it's likely you'll feel a little bit of fear because of the time you spent away. Does this make sense? The more time you spend away from a subject the less comfortable you'll be when you return. Depending on your level of commitment and practise it will be easier for some more than others to regain confidence once they have returned. Let me give you an example of what an old high school teacher once said to me on the subject of public speaking. "After a 6-week summer break from the classroom I return the first lesson back I feel this small amount of fear just before starting but soon after I begin teaching the fear goes again" This is a man who works a third of his life spent standing up in front of an audience speaking, when I heard him say that I was a little surprised, to say the least. But it proves to us that no matter how comfortable you get speaking in public the fear can always come back.

The fear will help you develop yourself

If you have read many self-development books then you'll understand what many people teach which is that fear just means you are going in a direction you have never gone before, that direction is where fear is present and all that stands for is uncertainty. It's because you have never done it before and you don't know what will happen. However, the more you do it eventually you'll feel more certain about it and more comfortable once you've reached a certain point the only way to grow and feel the fear is to challenge yourself more so present to a larger audience, spend more time on stage or deliver a more challenging speech. If you are to grow as a person, then you have to constantly live life at the end of your comfort zone and if you do this you are surely growing if you are not then you are not growing and if you are not **growing** then the opposite is true you are **dying.** So next time you feel the fear in a public speaking environment then that means there is potential for growth, What I'm trying to get across here is that the more often you feel uncomfortable doing something the more you'll grow and develop yourself as a person. Obviously, this won't happen overnight but you'll soon see the difference if you keep practising.

Where do I start?

So what is the best way to start public speaking? The answer will be different for everyone the simple answer is to start from where you are now. Speak up more in class. Take a leadership role in meetings at work, participate more in community organisations by adding your input. If you are often finding yourself in an environment where the same people are always taking charge or adding their input but you are not, then by stepping up I'm sure others will be grateful for it. If this isn't really an option for you right now, then there is an area outside of work and daily routines where you can improve your communication skills. That is by joining a public speaking class, if you live in an urban area the chances are there is one close by, take 5 minutes out of your day and look it up see if this is the case. I myself found a club known as toastmasters, this is a club devoted to excellence in public speaking. I would suggest everybody looking to improve this part of their life to join some sort of speaking organisation. If a public speaking club is not for you then it doesn't have to be a public speaking group but just some sort of club where communication is widely encouraged. A book club is one example here all members will generally share their favourite books through conversation and group chat but you could join a dance/sports club. While this is not exactly a public speaking environment it does require some form of verbal participation. If you don't feel the necessity join some form of club or you don't live in a geographically ideal location where it's easy for you to find these types of clubs, then volunteer or add input in your working environment. You'll often find teachers and employers will encourage this type of participation from time to time and will certainly be grateful for the responses they receive. One personal example comes to mind from a toastmaster's session where we were practising in improv, here 6 people would be asked to speak at the front for 1-2 minutes about a random subject. The first 4 participants were picked but the **5th** person was asked to volunteer nobody immediately volunteered so I volunteered, immediately I could tell people were grateful for this they even congratulated me in person once the session was over? Why did they do this? Well, the people who were most confident on stage were the ones who always volunteered always took up the leadership roles so everybody was accustomed to the same voices every, so when it came to me volunteering it was a new voice and face coming into the mix. Think about it if you don't engage much in the classroom or at work by doing so I'm sure it will be a good mix up to everybody listening. I'm not saying you are going to be guaranteed a positive response for volunteering like this but I'm sure your teacher or employer will be grateful for this not to mention you'll be noticed more. I've lost count how many times I've been inside a classroom, meeting room or lecture hall where the teacher/leader has asked for participation from the audience but only received limited engagement and if you notice always from the same people. More often than not this is because a fair number of the people sitting there may feel apprehensive about speaking up; I myself am guilty of this a hundred times over. Keeping your opinion may be the easier thing to do at the moment but by no stretch of the imagination will this serve you in the long run. Speak up and feel the fear while you do it, it won't kill you and it won't take 30 seconds to voice your opinion & I all but promise you'll feel better for doing so.

Someone else's opinion of you doesn't have to hold you back

Maybe it's not so much fear but what people will think of you that is hindering your ability to speak up, to be honest, anybody else's opinion does not play any role in your success or sense of happiness in life unless you allow it. What I've come to learn in life about criticism is that the only way to avoid this is to do nothing, say nothing and be nothing. You'll never be able to make everybody happy & nor should you try to. By trying to please other people, you'll never be able to do this consistently and in the end if won't work and it won't make you truly happy. Another thing to understand is that everybody is mainly focused on themselves, as harsh as this may sound you will never be the centre of everybody's attention. Even if you are on stage and you have everybody's attention this will never be permanent. In truth, a lot of people are thinking or worrying about their selves and when they are doing that little to no attention is focused on you. So don't worry about it and more often than not this will not be a problem anyway. I hope you enjoyed this chapter on fear hopefully by now this will motivate you to take action regardless of how fearful you feel about public speaking.

Chapter 16: Technicalities

Mindset is at the heart of professional and confident speaking. When you change how you approach the talk and its preparation, you can eliminate your fear and improve audience connection and your ability to improvise and deal with the unexpected.

The technicalities of speaking combine with the mindset work to make a powerful combination. Here we look at the important technical considerations of public speaking.

Eye contact

Eye contact is always difficult. Too little and the audience don't feel connected, too much and you come across a little strange.

So, what is the perfect amount of eye contact?

Scanning the audience throughout your talk is the starting point. From left to right and front to back, look at everyone in the audience (if you can see them) As you scan the audience you will naturally catch people's eyes - it's at that moment you maintain eye contact with them - only for a few seconds, or whilst you're making your point, then you go back to scanning and to catch someone else's eye.

Exercise

In a public setting, such as at the shops or on public transport, scan your surroundings and notice all the people you can see.

As you naturally will catch someone's eye (male or female) maintain the eye contact for a few short moments and notice at what point you begin to feel uncomfortable.

If the person responds negatively or asks you what you are doing you tell them, you thought you recognised them or they look like someone you know.

Simple.

Principles, not notes

When you give a talk on any topic, it needs to be something you believe in and something you are knowledgeable about.

If you prefer to have some structure, or need it to stay on track then it's advisable to use principles and bullet points rather than verbatim notes.

One of the reasons speakers can lose their thread and freeze on stage is because they are rigidly sticking to a plan and aiming for perfection. If you are following a specific plan and veer of course you feel lost and it can potentially destroy the rest of your talk.

By speaking in principles and having a looser structure (achievable when you are very familiar with your content) you can remain responsive in your delivery and if you do veer off track you can return to the rough plan you have rather than rigid verbatim notes.

Stage management

Stage management is the professional way of saying where you should stand and how you should move about when delivering your talk.

Traditional public speaker training encourages you to move from one side of the stage to the other, using it as a timeline for telling stories and "anchoring" certain parts which you return to when you talk about certain things.

We believe you should treat the stage as your home. No need to "anchor" or to do anything complicated.

Standing with broad shoulders and flat feet in a relaxed state is the best advice.

Speed

The speed at which you talk says a lot about your confidence.

Most people speak too quickly which is driven by their increased heart rate and Caveman thinking that they are in mortal danger, about to be eaten alive.

Those who speak more slowly and in a more considered way command more attention and come across as authorities in their given subject.

It's easy to say "slow down" when someone speaks quickly, but harder to internalise as you forget this when you feel a heightened sense of danger (even if it's not real danger)

The only way to beat the speed problem is to focus on delivering the words themselves:

Exercise

This exercise works as it gets you to focus on speaking clearly and pronunciation which removes your focus from "oh my god what do the audience think of me" to the technicalities of delivering some perfect "speaking"

Red leather, yellow leather...

Red lorry, yellow lorry...

You know New York,

You need New York,

You know you need unique New York.

Peter Piper picked a peck of pickled peppers.

A peck of pickled peppers Peter Piper picked.

If Peter Piper picked a peck of pickled peppers,

Where's the peck of pickled peppers Peter Piper picked?

Facts and figures

Facts and figures are a great way to demonstrate your knowledge and experience your chosen topic.

Proceed with caution.

Too many facts and figures can bore the audience and disconnect them as you move towards a more theoretical realm of speaking rather than connecting with the audience on an emotional and real level.

There are various different views on how many facts and figures to use, but the best way to decide for yourself is to consider what you want your audience to remember.

From experience the fewer the better.

Example

I heard a great talk on diabetes, given by an aspiring professional speaker, about how it is one of the world's largest killers, there were numerous astonishing facts and figures being quote, but one stayed with me.

- 1 in 16 people in the UK have diabetes, many of whom don't realise they have it.

WOW.

This fact resonated as I connected with it, I wondered if I was one of the 16, or someone close to me was.

This is what you need to look for. What are the key takeaways from your talk? Is there a single fact or figure that really connects and surmises your point?

Ask questions

Asking questions can invigorate a talk, but equally they can alienate the audience.

You will need to be clear if the question is rhetorical or not as you may get answers shouted at you randomly which can interrupt the flow of your talk.

A show of hands or a rhetorical question is a great way to relate to the audience and have them identify with your message.

Example

Asking questions engages the audience and brings their attention back to the stage, the following are great beginnings to connecting questions to ask the audience.

- Who here has ever felt...
- Who here has ever experienced...

- Does anyone know what it's like to...
- Would you ever think about...?
- What would you do if...
- Do you know anyone who has...?

Notice the questions focus on feeling, experience and real life.

We are looking for the audience to tap into their experiences and emotions, and to then connect that with your talk.

Commands

Commands are a useful way to connect with the audience and establish your authority.

It's astonishing how many people comply with your requests simply because you are at the front of the room giving a talk.

Types of command:

- Raise of hands.
- Shout out suggestions
- Stand up

- Sit down
- Shake hands / connect with neighbours
- Close eyes
- Clapping and noise making for atmosphere

Commands help to break the patterns to the room; help inject energy and refresh attention levels.

Exercise

Asking other people to do things in an authoritative way can be uncomfortable to begin with.

Asking strangers for the time, or for people to move aside on public transport are a great place to start.

Making requests in restaurants and asking others to bring you things or do small things for you can help to desensitise you and make requests feel far more normal.

Structure

There are many different ways to structure a talk, but we find the starting point is the only rigid part, we recommend starting with three things:

- Who you are
- Why you are here
- A Command

These are the three most important parts of the talk's structure.

Who you are is the most important opener, you aren't so much explaining who you are, as you are explaining why the audience should listen to you and what you have to say.

Why you are there is essentially your goal for the talk.

The command is engaging with the audience at the earliest possible point. The command can be a show of hands, asking the audience to close their eyes, to stand, to do anything which you request and is relevant for your talk.

For example:

- Hi guys, I'm Margaret Tate, I'm an international mindset coach.

- I'm here today to talk about removing the fear of public speaking.

- Can I ask by show of hands how many people are terrified of public speaking?

It's a simple as that.

Exercise

Create a strong opening structure for your talk which you can use time and again.

Firstly, who you are. Who you are (why you are relevant) can depend on your audience but being able to introduce yourself and what you do in a succinct and well-rehearsed way is a great asset for future talks.

Why you are giving the talk isn't always something you can prepare in advance, but if you generally speak on the same topics to the same kinds of crowds, then preparing a succinct and well-rehearsed "why" will help establish a clear objective with the audience.

Improvisation

Some of the best public speaking moments are unplanned.

Your ability to handle the unexpected and truly speak without notes is one of the most powerful assets as a speaker.

When you can improvise, you can connect the dots in a way which is relevant and meaningful for your audience.

The ability to improvise is a huge confidence boost as it's reassuring to know that whatever happens you can speak without notes on any given subject for at least a minute.

Exercise

Whilst either filming yourself or practising with a loved one, pick random subjects based on letters of the alphabet and talk about them for one minute a piece. See how far into the alphabet you can go.

For example, the letter A, the first thing which comes to mind is Apple so you'd need to talk for one minute on apples- what they are, where they come from, apple pie, apple juice etc.

Next up, letter B, the first thing that comes to mind is balloon. I would talk about using balloons to celebrate, helium balloons, hot air balloons and so on.

Another great exercise is to use a random noun generator to give you two seemingly unconnected words and you have to connect them in some way for 30-60 seconds.

Practise

This is the key to speaking excellence.

Practise.

You may not have the ability to give "real" talks often, depending on your circumstances, but that should not stop you from speaking often.

From talking to yourself in the mirror or in the car, filming yourself and playing it back, speaking to your friends, children, family, colleagues- it's a great chance to get feedback and to find your style.

If you are delivering a specific talk then there is no limit on how much you can or should practice to ensure it's the best it can be.

All of the mindset and technical pointers in this book

are meaningless unless you practise them.

Repetition

If an audience member asks a question, then the first thing you must always do is to repeat the question. This demonstrates that you understand the question being asked to avoid misunderstanding, buys you some time to consider your answer and helps those who may not have heard the question to hear it again before you respond.

When you make a key point in your talk, repeating the point a couple of times can ensure it is heard and understood. In the real world, repeating yourself seems odd, but on stage as a speaker, hearing someone repeat themselves is a clear marker which says "this is important"

Repetition is also a great way to manage the pace of your talk and how much content you are getting across. Stopping to repeat a point makes you and the audience slow down, rewind and then reconsider which is a powerful way to "underline" the important points you want to convey.

Don't talk straight away

One of the biggest mistakes you can make as a speaker is to jump on stage and jump straight into your talk.

The key difference between professional talks, TED talks and those who clearly are speaking for the first time is this:

Professional speakers take a moment at the start of their talk

to be silent and to "take in" the room.

This isn't to say you stand there for an uncomfortably long period of time, but taking even 2 or 3 seconds to stand there and to settle in to the stage can encourage the audience to believe you are in control, are confident and are deliberate in all that you do.

Thank you

Always end with a thank you.

The audience have sat there patiently listening to you speaking for the last few minutes, so remember to always recognise this with a sincere and heartfelt thank you.

A sincere thank is always the perfect end to a speech and leaves the audience with a great "last impression" of you as a polite and considerate speaker.

Typically, the audience will remember what you looked like, perhaps one or two key points, but most importantly how you made them feel. By showing gratitude you make the audience feel appreciated and valued.

Chapter 17: Getting Started

While donating your public speaking can help build experience, I don't recommend doing that as a general practice.

Speaking for Free -- Is it a Good Idea?

If you do feel more comfortable starting out without payment, consider practicing **within a group where the focus is on practice** -- as in a Toastmasters chapter -- or even starting your own. (The beauty of starting your own? You can set up an online practice group!)

Yes, introducing other speakers is another good way to become comfortable with being the (brief) center of attention -- and making notes about what works and what doesn't, for yourself. But volunteer or agree to donate your services for free and you may find yourself never considered for the "paying gigs".

When you have at least three paid gigs under your belt, then you can consider donating your public speaking time... providing it's for a specific, worthy cause.

You can also agree to exchange guest appearances on a business peer's webinar, for example. Or agree to form part of a panel or teach a workshop **in exchange for the right to record, re-purpose and sell** your appearance to your own list.

Finally, another time you might want to donate your time -- if organizers are "stuck" with a failed presenter and they beg you to bail them out. In which case, make sure you've decided on a policy -- will you ask for payment? (Easy formula: "I'm assuming you'll pay me the same rate as [Failed Presenter] -- how and when will that payment be made?") Is it a non-profit workshop? (Simply ask, if you don't know.)

The main thing to remember, when deciding whether or not to speak for free, is that in some way, there has to be reciprocity to it -- even if that's just making the right connections -- or you will not win respect as a professional (and you won't feel good about being "used".)

Toastmasters

Toastmasters is a non-profit group with chapters (clubs) in almost every country. Its mission is to help people improve communication and leadership skills. Public speaking is a major tool they use. Membership is open to anyone over eighteen who is interested in improving their communication skills -- though they do provide "Gavel clubs" for teenagers in some areas.

Each chapter meets anywhere from once a week to once a month and their philosophy involves "learning by doing". There is a manual and specific speaking techniques to learn, and each member is expected (after training) to present a speech of between five to seven minutes in length at meetings. (There is also a leadership manual.)

Many a glossophobe has got their trembling start at Toastmasters. Everyone

I've spoken to who is a member has (a) quickly conquered their fear of public speaking (b) loudly sung the organization's praises.

Their website allows you to input your city or zip code and instantly find Toastmasters clubs near you.

Storytelling Schools

Another way to become comfortable with public speaking is to take a storytelling course, if one is available in your area. The drawback to this is that most storytelling courses are paid, which might not work for you if you are on a shoestring budget. Plus they are not as widespread as toastmasters.

But storytelling is an essential part of connecting with your audience -- no matter how dry or technical your subject -- so don't underestimate its value!

I've given presentations and told stories publicly: And I can attest that if you can tell a successful story to any age group in any venue, mere presentations pale in comparison!

Simply enter the keywords: "Storytelling courses" + [your city], to find out what's available in your area.

Starting Your Own Group

The ideal time to start your own group is after you've taken that storytelling course -- if you're going to have to be the leader and organizer.

But having a peer-based group, in which the only formality is meeting time and place, plus length of speech, will work even for the most inexperienced would-be presenter... providing you can find others interested in honing their skills too.

One tip, however: **Limit the number of members**. Do the math, to decide on your ideal number. Are you meeting for an hour? Figure on five minutes for chit-chat while you wait for late arrivals and warm up the "room". (Be there at least fifteen minutes early, if you're the leader, so you can also chat with early arrivals!) Add another five minutes for issuing a welcome and introducing the day's topics. Figure on another five minutes for wrap-up... and that's fifteen minutes out of your hour, leaving you with forty five minutes. If you divide that segment into five minutes per person (three minutes for a speech, two for feedback or comments) your maximum membership ought to be nine members.

How to Let People Know -- If you're planning a location-based group in a physical room, your local newspaper is the place to start. Send out a **press release**, as well as a separate, short notification for **community events**.

1. Be sure to date your submissions

2.Be sure to put your release date on your press release

3.Remember your press release has to be a newsworthy story -- try to find a single angle most likely to attract the people you want

4.**Make sure you address** what, where, why, when, how (much) **and** who

Your **local library** or **business organizations** are also idea places to place announcements.

Be sure to state that only the first [X] will be able to sign up, if you are planning on limiting it to a small group. If you are planning an online group, announcing it in your forums, on your Facebook page, via Google+ or other social networks ought to be enough.

Send personal invitations to list members or business peers you would like to see in your group.

Again, be sure to state that membership will be limited.

How to Get Started as a Speaker

And now the segment you've probably been waiting for... how to actually get started!

1. **Know your goal** -- what do you want your public speaking career to do for you? (Providing a source of income we'll take as a given.) Do you want to educate potential clients? Position yourself as an expert? Become famous? Change the world? Help people achieve personal success and self-actualization? Teach them a skill? Attract subscribers? Appear on national TV?

2. **Make sure you specialize in a topic you will never get tired of** -- one you are passionate about or one that you thoroughly enjoy.

3.**Search your local library** -- Libraries will have listings of meetings and events. Make a note of these organizations and contact them, if you think they're the perfect fit for your subject.

4.**Ask for referrals** -- At the end of your presentation, be bold about asking your audience to recommend you to other groups they think would like your services. Point out your business cards (on display, along with other promotional materials, I hope!)

Put your referral request right on your business card!

5.**Use Testimonials** -- Put them right on your website, once you begin to become known. An honest testimonial that's heartfelt can easily land you a paid speaking gig -- even if the hirer has never seen you speak.

Who Can You Speak For?

This starts with your subject -- your specialty? What would you never get tired of talking about? Once you've got your topic, you've got your audience.

Look for local organizations that would most benefit from your services -- and approach them. Have dedicated business cards for your public speaking already made up. Online, it's easy to Google speaker directories and look for candidates that are a good fit:

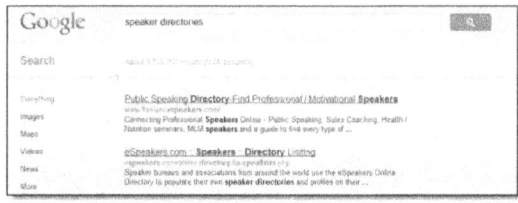

As you can see, there over nine million to choose from. (TIP: Add your specific niche keyword to narrow down the results.)

But first, check out Speaker Services and Speaker Zone. (The latter is an especially good source of resource tips and materials!)

And for those who want to speak online, a great way to get started is to check out: Lunchinars.

Putting On Your Own Events

If you belong to even one or two local niche or business organizations, you can plan your own event -- paid or free -- and publicize it with ease. (Just remember to ask people to pass on the information, and have your brochures or business cards ready.)

If you're worried that people won't pay to come to your event, invite a "core" group as special guests. Even if no one else shows up, you can "practice" presenting to this group, ask for testimonials from them -- and repurpose your content, if you were savvy enough to record the event and/or have it transcribed.

Reward "Special Guests" Who Attend -- Be sure to reward your special guests! The minimum would be a personal thank-you note, but you can add gift cards for local restaurants, copies of your books if you have any or any other bonus you think they would enjoy.

You can also put on an online event, and publicize it through your usual channels -- forums you belong to (if allowed); social networks; your blog; your website; sales or squeeze pages; press releases; requests for word-of-mouth recommendations, etc.)

Your Website -- Setting Up a Media Page -- If you're going to send out press releases and set yourself up as a speaker, you should also have:

A website focusing strictly on your public speaking career

A media page, where people hiring you can pick up professional-quality, full-sized photos, bio blurbs and more

How Much Should You Charge? -- That's really up to you. (The correct answer is really "whatever the market will bear!")

Here are some tips you can put to good use:

1. **Check out your competition**. What do similarly-experienced peers who specialize in public speaking? Look up their rates, and set yours accordingly.

2. **How much experience have you had?** The more public presentations you've given the more you can usually charge -- with confidence

3. **How much value are you bringing to the event?** If someone else is organizing it, how big a draw will your name be?

4. Factor in your time, event-specific expenses, travel, food and accommodation costs **-- and charge at least double for that as your base line**

5. **How much value is the event bringing you**? If the possibility of creating new, profitable relationships or spreading your reach is particularly alluring, you may feel it's worthwhile to settle for less than your usual fee or even put yourself out of pocket

To put this all into perspectives, $2,500 is the lowest fee large corporations or companies would expect you to work for.

If you are invited to speak by a local organization or company, they might feel a couple of hundred is a huge bite out of their budget.

If you are invited to speak by a non-profit organization, they'll most likely expect you to donate your time!

What to Speak About

It doesn't matter what you speak about, as long as:

It fits into your main mission and supports your goal

It is tailored to your audience and their goals

You stick to one basic theme or angle

For example, if your workshop is all about how to create a business plan, it would actually weaken your "lesson" if you suddenly went off on a tangent and began speaking about setting up Autoresponders or how to hire the best bookkeepers.

If you get a question that's not relevant to the subject, acknowledge the question ("That's a good question...") and firmly table it to another time that won't disrupt the presentation.

Here are three ways to gracefully turn the conversation back to business:

"...Be sure to remind me after the presentation, during the question and answer period"

"...However, we don't have time to cover that in this presentation. Speak to me after the presentation, and I'll point you to some resources."

"...But we're here today to speak about Adobe Photoshop, so unfortunately we need to keep to that topic."

Gauge your audience. Remember that you are only half the event: Your audience completes it. Together, you make the event become an entity in its own right, with a soul and a persona. It can be absolutely magical to see this transformation -- as if the event comes alive, and you're just there to facilitate.

Each speaking engagement will feel different because your audience will be different. Learn to read their moods and needs, and you can be as direct as you please.

How to Craft a Talk That Sells

There's a specific process for coming up with a strong presentation. All of these elements should be present -- even if you mix them up into an order that feels more natural to you.

1. Define your topic and angle

2. **Analyze your audience.** (What does your audience need? What are they there for?)

3. **Analyze their communication style**. (Will they respond better to a dry, technical presentation? To humor?

Anecdotes? Fast paced? Are they visual learners? Will metaphors turn them off or help them better understand your points?)

4.**Write your skeleton** -- the key points you have to cover to get from beginning to end

5.**Think of new, original ways to cover these points**. Is there new information you can share? A unique short-cut? Powerful resources to introduce them to? A revolutionary approach?

6.**Look for ways to connect emotionally with your audience**. What will make them sit up? Visualize themselves in your place? See you in their place?

7.**Decide what visual aids you are going to use**. (Handouts, slide shows, Power Point presentations). Ask yourself: "Why? Is this the best way to show this point? Will it break their concentration or perk them up?"

8.**Write your introduction**. Remember to make it dynamic.

9. **Write your conclusion** -- make sure it includes a call to action (your request for referrals, an invitation to sign up for your next event or fill out a short survey, etc.) If possible, refer to your opening in your conclusion for maximum impact ("completing the circle"). And, if possible, finish with a rousing, positive, "feel good" statement they can carry away with them.

10. **Fill in the middle**. At this point, this will probably feel like the easiest part!

11. Proof your speech, print it out and read it aloud **at least three times.**

12. Notice where your tongue "trips" over words **and rewrite that sentence or section**

13. **Practice** until the speech fits you like a glove.

How to Position Yourself So They're Eager to Pay You

It's good to be vulnerable and human, but if you want to be seen as a "catch" worth paying good money in the world of public speaking, there are definite dos and don'ts.

1. **Never, ever apologize for being there!** You'd be surprised the number of people who begin presentations by saying self-deprecating things like: "I've no idea why so-and-so asked me to speak about coffee makers, but here I am!"

2. **Don't use jargon**. No one wants to hear about inferred primordial abundances unless they are physicists! And if you use an acronym, let people know what it means, the first time you use it. ("Now RADA -- the Royal Academy of Dramatic Arts -- maintains that...")

Using jargon is akin to "putting your audience to sleep"! And if you've attracted international audience members (which happens more than you think, if you're presenting online) you may totally confuse them.

3. **Never worry about "looking good"** -- Instead, eagerly anticipate sharing

4.**Deliver more than they expect** -- Whether that's new insider information, a fresh outlook that finally helps them make sense of a difficult subject, handouts or free samples, make sure you pack as much focused value as you can into your presentation -- all aimed to:

Thrill your audience

Make your hosts "look good" -- they're the heroes that brought you in!

5.**Eliminate the Umms and Ahhs** -- Recording yourself is the best way to identify what your particular annoying "filler" noises and phrases are. For instance, when I first heard myself speak on tape, I was appalled at how many times I said "Basically". (I don't think I've said it since!)

Once you've identified them, do your best to erase them from your speeches.

6.**Be dependable** -- Arrive on time (check out the location in advance, if it's a physical location). Don't depend on your hosts for "extra" equipment -- have everything you need with you... or else have a back up plan! And never, ever cancel, if you can help it.

7. Realize you're being paid for your perceived value -- Not just your experiences and expertise. If you're speaking about Barbie dolls to an accountant's convention, your perceived value might easily be zero (and nobody would know -- or care -- "who" you are): If you're speaking to the Barbophiles of the San Fernando Valley, however -- and they are excited by the fact that you're the original designer of the "Francie" wig -- your perceived value may be priceless.

Similarly, if you're the one person whose talk can boost productivity in a failing department almost immediately by thirty percent, you'll also be priceless!

While people naturally want guest who are celebrities, most are quite aware their budgets won't stretch to Bill Clinton (who, when last heard of commanded $150,000 for a one-hour speaking engagement).

They want someone who is:

Well respected in their niche

Dependable

Available!

Simply **being willing to speak** and **doing so in a professional, enjoyable manner** automatically positions you as a niche leader and expert.

You'll build your reputation more quickly than you think!

Chapter 18: Fear Technology

Are there natural born speakers? The answer is debatable. One thing is certain, though; speaking in front of a large group can be learned. Do you ever wonder why experts of communication are so natural on stage? Do they experience some degree of stage fright at all? The answer is yes!

Fear in itself is in fact a performance enhancer. It improves memory and decision-making skills. The aim is not the absolute expulsion of the feeling but the management of it.

Evolutionary psychologists explained that the dreaded feeling was rooted a long time ago. We evolved as social beings because our chances of survival in groups are ultimately higher than those of survival alone. With others, defense against large predators and gathering food are easier while being ejected from the group is almost certain death. That's why we carry the instinct of fear of rejection. We always want to belong in a group. Fast forward to the present, there are many instances that the instinct is triggered and one of them is speaking in front of the people.

Whether you are in a band that has played a thousand gigs before or a professor who has given lots of lectures, you are sure to experience fear every time you step on stage. Why? It's because fear is normal! However, the key is in how you manage it.

Control your fear by acknowledging it. Then ask yourself "So what's making me afraid?" For example, "I think I'll stutter as I greet them." Then realize that they're all just products of procrastination. Combat this by realizing that those thoughts repeating in your head have no use and are just making you nervous. Convert your thoughts into positive ones like "I practiced so hard so I know I can do this" or "I'm getting this done and getting promoted."

This kind of thinking is called cognitive behavioral therapy. CBT basically follows the notion that thoughts influence behavior. This technique has been recognized by many psychologists to be the best management for fear especially stage fright.

Do deep breathing exercises on top of this method. The physical signs of anxiety include increased heart rate, sweaty palms, and the so-called butterflies in the stomach. By simply staying calm (through CBT) and breathing deeply and slowly, you can surely possess an unstoppable confidence!

Conclusion

Thank you again for downloading this book!

I hope this book was able to help you to become more at ease with the idea of speaking in public. Soon enough, you will realize that it's not as bad as it seems. You only needed to be equipped with the right knowledge in order to face the battle with words as your weapon head-on.

I hope you learned techniques you can utilize in order to overcome those horrible bats in your stomach whenever you're about to speak. Bear in mind as well the elements that you must take into consideration as you prepare to deliver your presentation. Furthermore, public speaking will end up failing if you don't take the important practices that you must observe seriously when you finally speak in front of your listeners.

With all the benefits public speaking can offer, I hope you have come to acknowledge how important it is to hone your communication and public speaking skills. Hopefully with the guidance of this book, you can ultimately find yourself at center stage.

The next step is to apply the instructions in this book and take them to heart. Moreover, remember that to become more at ease with speaking, you need to do it again and again. Every time you give a speech, the stage fright and all your apprehension becomes easier to deal with. And you will also have experiences in your arsenal from which to draw insights. If you limit yourself to speaking only when it's necessary, you won't gain mistakes that you can learn from and much more positive experiences to gain a confidence boost. Speaking is no different from other skills. Take swimming for example. You can read a how-to manual about breaststrokes and freestyles, about the techniques to hold your breath under water, and swim like the greatest mermaid who has ever lived, but if you don't get into the water and swim, you will never learn. The same principle goes for public speaking. If there are opportunities to refine your skills, take them.

Thank you for reading to the end!

www.ingramcontent.com/pod-product-compliance
Lightning Source LLC
Chambersburg PA
CBHW071845080526
44589CB00012B/1118